E-MAIL
A WRITE IT WELL GUIDE
How to Write and Manage E-Mail in the Workplace

By Janis Fisher Chan

Write It Well

Published by Write It Well
Post Office Box 13098, Oakland, CA 94661
Phone: (510) 655-6477 Fax: (510) 291-9744
www.writeitwell.com

Acknowledgements:

Contributing Editor – Natasha Terk

Book design – freshbait, a creative company

Typography – John Richards

ISBN 13: 978-0-9637455-9-0

Second edition, January 2008

To order this book:
Visit our Web site, www.writeitwell.com, or your favorite bookstore

*For Diane, who loved communication
in all its forms.*

CONTENTS

Since we published the first edition of this book in 2005, the use of e-mail for business communications has become routine. People now check their e-mail as often—or more often—than they check for voicemail messages. More and more people are reading and writing e-mail on mobile, or hand-held, devices, such as cell phones and BlackBerries, and increasing numbers are routinely using instant Messaging (IM) in the workplace to hold real-time "conversations" with colleagues, clients, and others.

"Business writing" and "e-mail" have become more or less synonymous terms. Nearly all interoffice memos are now sent as e-mail. E-mail is commonly used in place of "hard copy" letters to communicate with clients and others outside an organization. The ability to reach many people with a few keystrokes makes e-mail the most convenient choice for disseminating information about almost anything. It's easier than ever to send documents of all types and sizes to recipients all over the world.

The advances in electronic communication are rapidly changing the way we work. Not least, it is becoming far easier for increasing numbers of people to work remotely—while traveling, from home, and as part of virtual teams. But the same advances have also created significant problems: We're now expected to be reachable at all times, no matter where we are, which makes it very hard to get away from our work; the ability to read and write e-mail from almost anywhere has decreased response speed, raising the expectations for a speedy response; it's easier than ever to send inappropriate or sensitive information to the wrong people; and the permanent record created by electronic communication is increasingly being used as evidence in legal actions.

Over the past two years, hundreds of articles and several books have appeared with advice and guidance for this ubiquitous but still relatively new form of communication. Yet the same old issues keep e-mail use from being as productive as it could be. People still send e-mail that is confusing, conveys an unprofessional image, offends others, or lands them and their organizations in court. They waste valuable time writing e-mail that doesn't need to be sent, trying to keep up with an overloaded inbox, or searching for lost messages that contain crucial information. They interrupt themselves and annoy others by constantly checking for new mail while they're in the middle of important tasks, in meetings, or out on dinner dates.

Here's one thing we've learned: Like any other job-related task, using e-mail productively requires thought and attention. We wrote the original edition of this book to help you do that. Because electronic communication is now being used even more and in more ways, we've updated some topics, such as the use of attachments, and added some information, such as that on instant messaging and using e-mail with hand-held devices. We hope these changes make the book even more useful as you struggle to find productive ways of writing and managing your e-mail in the workplace.

Good luck!

INTRODUCTION

The more electronic and global we get, the less important the spoken word has become, and in e-mail, clarity is critical.

— SEAN PHILLIPS, APPLERA CORPORATE RECRUITMENT DIRECTOR
IN "WHAT CORPORATE AMERICA CAN'T BUILD: A SENTENCE"
THE NEW YORK TIMES, DECEMBER 7, 2004

WHY THIS BOOK

Electronic mail has become the dominant method of communication for people in the workplace. We use e-mail to communicate with team members, clients, customers, and vendors; we even use it when we have a question for a colleague down the hall. More of us are using e-mail to stay in touch with the office while traveling or working from home. And our participation in the growing global economy means that we use e-mail to communicate more frequently with people in other countries and time zones.

Our e-mail use is only likely to increase. Eighty per cent of the people who responded to a 2003 META Group survey of 387 organizations believed that e-mail is more useful than the phone.[1] Recent surveys conducted by the American Management Association and the e-Policy Institute reveal that we now spend between 30 minutes and four hours—or more—a day on e-mail-related activities. An October 2006 report by technology market research firm The Radicati Group estimates that some 183 billion emails were sent each day in 2006 and that wireless email users will grow "from 14 million in 2006, to 228 million in 2010."[2]

There's no question that e-mail is an invaluable tool for doing business. Yet reading, writing, and managing e-mail is taking an increasing amount of our time, and we don't always use that time productively. That's why we've written this book: to provide information, ideas, and strategies for making the best use of your e-mail time and making sure that the e-mail you write gets the results you want.

WHY WE USE E-MAIL

There are good reasons that e-mail has become the primary method of communication in the workplace. It's an incredibly efficient and inexpensive way of exchanging information. Still, the use—and misuse—of e-mail has also created lots of problems.

What Makes E-Mail Valuable

When used appropriately, e-mail lets us do the following:

- Reduce "phone tag" when communicating with people who are hard to reach on the telephone

- Convey information and get responses to questions more quickly, easily, and informally than by mailing a letter or sending a standard interoffice memo

- By using attachments, send documents over long distances in moments rather than days, and at a lower cost

- Keep a lot of people informed by providing an easy means of getting the same message across to many people at once

- Reduce the need for meetings where the only purpose is to share information

- Communicate efficiently with people who work in other locations, especially those in other time zones

- Make better decisions by involving more people in the process of generating ideas and providing information

- Maintain a written record of discussions, decisions, agreements, and the dissemination of information

Common Problems With E-Mail

Used inappropriately or inefficiently, however, e-mail can create serious problems for us, as individuals, and for our organizations. Common problems include:

- Reduced productivity resulting from unplanned, poorly written messages that fail to convey information clearly

- Loss of credibility resulting from sloppily written messages that contain errors in grammar, punctuation, and spelling

- Offensive content and tone that damage relationships and can result in lawsuits

- Loss of confidentiality when e-mail is used to convey private or proprietary information

- Misunderstandings that occur because the body language, facial expressions, and tone of voice that help people interpret a communication are missing

- Time wasted writing, reading, and responding to e-mail that did not need to be sent, searching for lost messages, or compulsively checking for new mail

ABOUT THIS BOOK

We've designed *E-Mail: A Write It Well Guide* to provide practical information, ideas, and strategies for using e-mail appropriately and productively in the workplace. It doesn't matter whether your workplace is a huge corporation or a small business, a professional office or a nonprofit organization, an academic institution or a government agency. It doesn't matter whether you're a customer service representative, a scientist, a marketing specialist, a supervisor or manager, an executive, an analyst, a professor, a consultant, or a business owner. The information in this book will help you write better e-mail messages and manage your e-mail more efficiently so you can be more productive and get better results.

Objectives

This book will help you:

- Write clear, concise e-mail that quickly conveys the information people need and gets the results you want

- Use your e-mail time more productively by improving your writing process; knowing when and to whom to send e-mail; and managing your e-mail efficiently

- Convey a professional image of yourself and your organization through the e-mail you send

- Avoid trouble by recognizing what topics and information are and are not appropriate for e-mail

If you're a human resources or training professional, or if you are responsible for establishing standards and guidelines for e-mail use in your organization, the information in this book will also help you:

- Design and conduct training
- Develop e-mail standards and enforce an e-mail policy

Chapter Overviews

Each of the five chapters includes explanations, examples, guidelines, tips, and questions to help you think about the ways in which you use e-mail. At the end of each chapter are suggestions for applying what you learn and pages on which we encourage you to note your own ideas for using e-mail more productively. At the back of the book, you'll find supplementary information and a guide to learning more.

Here's a quick look at what's in the book:

CHAPTER ONE. THINK BEFORE YOU WRITE. The key to clear writing is clear thinking. To write e-mail that communicates clearly to specific individuals and groups, you need to think about your purpose for writing, your audience, the message you want to convey, and what information your readers need. This chapter provides a step-by-step process for planning clear, concise e-mail messages that get results. It also includes suggestions for developing e-mail "templates" that can streamline the writing process; guidelines for reading and writing e-mail on hand-held devices; and suggestions for using Instant Messaging at work.

CHAPTER TWO. LAUNCHING YOUR MESSAGE. In some ways, sending an e-mail message is more complicated than putting a letter into an envelope. This chapter addresses common questions about getting messages ready to send, including making sure the message makes sense; checking the tone; selecting the right format, salutation, closing, and signature; using lists; sending attachments; writing a good subject line; and addressing the message.

CHAPTER THREE. MANAGING YOUR E-MAIL. As we send and receive an increasing amount of e-mail, we need efficient ways to manage our e-mail-related tasks. This chapter provides ideas and information that will help you set up schedules and systems for using your e-mail time as productively as possible. You'll learn how to keep e-mail from interrupting your work; decide when and how to respond to a message; keep your inbox from overflowing; and set up folders that help you quickly find the e-mail you need to see again.

CHAPTER FOUR. PRESENT A PROFESSIONAL IMAGE. Your written communications tell people a lot about you and your organization. E-mail that is filled with errors not only fails to communicate clearly, it conveys an image of someone who isn't paying much attention, doesn't value the correspondence, and might not have much knowledge. In this chapter, you'll review the use of active, specific, concise language and plain English, along with important rules of grammar and punctuation.

CHAPTER FIVE. CAUTIONARY TALES. It's a fact that putting the wrong information in an e-mail can have serious consequences: people can be offended or angered, confidential or private information can be unwittingly released, and organizations can find themselves in court. This chapter discusses the risks of using e-mail to convey certain kinds of information and the rights of organizations to monitor employees' e-mail. It also includes suggestions for setting up and enforcing policies to govern e-mail use.

THE BACK OF THE BOOK. We end the book with ideas for continuing to improve your writing, suggestions for learning more about e-mail, and a glossary of common e-mail terminology.

BEFORE YOU BEGIN

Below are a few things to keep in mind as you read this book:

E-MAIL IS WRITTEN COMMUNICATION. Even though e-mail has some unique characteristics, it's still writing, and the basics of clear writing are always the same. Everything you'll learn in these pages about planning and writing a clear, concise, professional e-mail message applies to all the writing you do.

USE THE BOOK THE WAY IT WORKS FOR YOU. Each chapter addresses one broad topic. You might want to read the book straight through and then use it as a reference. You might use it as a workbook, scribbling in the margins and using the Notes pages at the end of the chapters to record your own ideas for using e-mail more productively. You might use the Table of Contents to jump right to the topics that are of most interest to you.

THINK ABOUT WHAT YOU'RE READING. We've included questions to help you think about the material and suggested ways to apply what you learn to your e-mail tasks. You'll notice that some chapters are more "interactive" than others, because of the nature of the information. The most interactive is Chapter Four, "Present a Professional Image," which includes exercises to help you review the rules and guidelines for using clear, concise, correct language, grammar, and punctuation.

THIS BOOK IS NOT A TECHNICAL MANUAL. We haven't included detailed instructions for attaching documents to your e-mail messages, setting up your preferences, creating signature files, or filtering out spam. We haven't delved into the many technical topics associated with e-mail use for several reasons. We're not technical experts, for one thing; for another, many of the details would be old news before the book came off the press. What we have done is include suggestions for getting answers to technical questions.

YOU CAN USE THIS BOOK FOR TRAINING. If you're a manager, human resources professional, trainer, or team leader, you can use this book for learning programs that help people write effective e-mail and manage their e-mail time productively. See our Web site, www.writeitwell.com, for suggestions and resources, training guidelines, and instructor's guides that include sample learning program designs, suggested activities, practice exercises and quizzes.

YOU CAN USE THIS BOOK AS A RESOURCE FOR DEVELOPING E-MAIL STANDARDS. Every organization, large or small, needs an e-mail policy that tells people what's okay to do and what's not. The information in this book can help you develop writing standards and guidelines for e-mail use. Chapter Five discusses what to consider when developing an e-mail policy and how to communicate your policy to members of the group or organization. You'll find suggestions for learning more about e-mail policies on our Web site.

> **HOW DO YOU SPELL IT?**
>
> There are different ways to spell e-mail. The common forms are "e-mail," "email," and "emails." Because the word means "electronic mail," we've used the singular form with a hyphen: "e-mail" and "e-mail messages."

1 THINK BEFORE YOU WRITE

Some of the e-mail I get reads like someone's stream of consciousness, as if the writer just dumped whatever was in his or her head onto the computer screen. It would save me a lot of time and trouble if people would stop for a minute and think through what they want to say.

— JEFF ANGELL
PRESIDENT, PURA VIDA COFFEE

E-mail is ideal for the kinds of quick messages that most of us send in response to questions, to pass along information, and to make requests. We use e-mail *because* it's quick and easy—more like leaving a phone message than writing. It doesn't seem to take the same kind of thinking and planning time as writing a hard-copy memo, a letter, or a report.

But e-mail is still writing. Even if you have only a simple message to convey, you'll get better results if you stop and think about why you're writing, what information you want to pass along, and what you want the recipient to do. Unplanned messages like the one below waste everybody's valuable time:

> Maggie, you gave me a copy of an article a couple of weeks ago, when we had lunch at Zeke's, you know, that day my car broke down and I had to take the bus so I was late and you almost left? Can't remember exactly what it was, something from the Times or maybe the Post, all I remember is that it was one of our competitors talking about a new product. Anyway, I told my manager about it and he was really interested, wanted to know what it said and I said I'd look for it, but then I couldn't find it in my briefcase or anywhere. What I was wondering was whether you'd mind sending me a copy. Thanks a lot and I really enjoyed our lunch. Let's do it again soon.
>
> Brad

That message forces Maggie to waste time searching for the main point, and if she's in a rush, she could easily miss it. If Brad had taken a few moments to focus his thoughts before writing, the e-mail would be much more effective:

> Maggie,
>
> Would you mind sending me another copy of the article about our competitor's new product that you gave me when we had lunch at Zeke's? I seem to have lost it, and my manager would like to see it.
>
> Thanks a lot. I really enjoyed our lunch. Let's do it again soon.
>
> Brad

The revised message gets the point across more quickly and clearly. All it took was a little planning.

PLAN YOUR WRITING

Whether it's an e-mail message, a letter, a project report, or a marketing brochure, the key to clear writing is the *planning* you do before you begin. Planning means thinking about why you're writing, who you're writing to, what you want to say, and what results you expect.

No matter how pressed you are for time, it's worthwhile to ask these questions for every e-mail message you send:

- Is e-mail the appropriate choice for this message?
- Why am I writing this e-mail? What's my purpose?
- Who's my audience? What's my reader's point of view?
- What's the main point? What's the most important message?
- What information should I include? What does my reader need to know?
- What's the best way to organize the information?

Let's look more closely at each of those questions.

IS E-MAIL THE APPROPRIATE CHOICE FOR THIS MESSAGE?

What if you received the three e-mail messages below? Is e-mail the best way—or the right way—to communicate the information? Why or why not?

Dear Daniel,

This is to notify you that you have come in more than half an hour late four days out of the past seven. We spoke about this issue during your last performance evaluation. If you show up late one more time, I will be forced to institute disciplinary proceedings.

Sincerely,
Larissa

~

Hi, Sienna,

Thanks for filling in for me at the meeting yesterday—I owe you one. By the way, I heard that your manager is thinking about leaving the company. His daughter mentioned it to my daughter in gymnastics class. Better keep it to yourself for now, but I thought you'd like to know.

Byron

~

Billie,

I know how you feel about that invoice. I almost lost it and screamed at the finances woman, because she kept telling me she didn't have it. There seems to be some sort of vortex of doom around it because I can't find my copy either, and I know you sent me at least two of them. I feel like shooting myself in the face! I'm afraid to go down to Financial Services myself because at this stage I'd get in a fistfight. There is no reason this should be happening. Could you please fax me copies ONE MORE TIME? This will get solved today, or I start building a death-ray laser gun out of office supplies. I would rather quit than deal with this problem any more! It's become emblematic of my struggles with this organization's bureaucracy and with certain people's incompetence.

Sorry for the tirade,
Parker

You probably agree that e-mail was not the appropriate choice for any of those three messages. Larissa's message to Daniel addressed performance issues, which should always remain confidential and are best addressed face-to-face. Byron passed on a rumor, assuming that Sienna would keep it confidential. And Parker used e-mail to vent his feelings, something he might later regret.

Convenience is not a good enough reason for using e-mail to communicate certain kinds of information. E-mail is too public, for one thing—it's more like sending a postcard than sealing a letter into an envelope. It lacks the human interaction that facilitates communication. And you can't always control the way an e-mail message looks on your recipient's screen.

Consider the Consequences

To make sure that e-mail is the appropriate choice, think carefully about the possible consequences whenever you need to communicate the following:

CONFIDENTIAL OR PRIVATE INFORMATION. It's easy to think that only the person or people to whom we've addressed a message will see it. That's not necessarily true. As we discuss in Chapter Five, e-mail is a public medium, and there's always a chance that people other than your intended recipients will see an e-mail you send. Before putting your company's secret formula or an employee's medical history into an e-mail message, ask yourself what might happen if someone published that information in the newspaper.

> **IMAGINE THE CONSEQUENCES**
>
> **What if e-mail containing these remarks ended up in the wrong person's inbox?**
>
> . . . and Malcom is the positively WORST boss I've ever had—he's rude and petty, and he knows nothing about this business!
>
> ~
>
> . . . Keep this under your hat, but we're about to be bought out by. . . . it'll be a real shake-up around here but the stock should really take off. . . .

SENSITIVE TOPICS. E-mail is no substitute for a face-to-face conversation or a carefully worded memo or letter that only the recipient is likely to see. It offers none of the human interaction that is so vital when your message might upset the other person—for example, when you're criticizing someone's performance. Without the clues you get from facial expressions, body language, or tone of voice, you might not realize that what you've communicated is hurtful or offensive.

Also, we sometimes say things in e-mail that we would never say to someone on the phone or in person. It's all too easy to dump negative feelings into an e-mail message and send it off without rereading it or thinking about how the recipient might feel about it.

HUMOR. The casual quality of e-mail makes it easy to forget that it can be the wrong place for jokes or "funny" stories, especially those that poke fun at an individual or a group. Some of the things that seem funny to you could offend other people who happen to see the message. In addition to creating bad feelings, offensive e-mail can get you—and your organization—in a lot of trouble. See Chapter Five for details.

COMPLEX INFORMATION. The body of an e-mail is not usually the best way to convey complex information such as a detailed report. It's hard to read that kind of information on a screen. Your recipient is likely to print the message out, and software incompatibility can make it hard to control the way the printout looks. To preserve formatting and make the document more useful for the recipient, send it as an attachment to an e-mail that describes—and perhaps summarizes—its contents. (There's more about attachments in Chapter Two.)

How to Decide What's Appropriate

Here are some questions to help you decide whether the content you plan to communicate is appropriate for an e-mail:

- How would I feel if I received this kind of information in an e-mail?

- What might happen if someone other than my intended recipient receives this message?

- Would I actually say this on the phone or to this person's face?

- Is anyone liable to be offended by the content of this e-mail? Is it possible that this e-mail could become part of a legal action?

- Does my organization have any rules against this type of e-mail?

- Is my recipient likely to print out this message? Does the formatting need to be preserved?

THINK ABOUT . . .

Have you ever received an inappropriate e-mail? How did you feel about it? Did other people see it? Were there any consequences? Did it affect the business relationship?

Were any of the messages you sent within the last two weeks not appropriate for e-mail? What would have been a better way to communicate that information—or should it have been communicated at all?

WHAT'S MY PURPOSE?

Read this message quickly. Can you state the writer's purpose in a single sentence?

> To My Team,
>
> Thanks so much for all your hard work during the past six months! We would never have exceeded our goals without your efforts, creativity, and enthusiasm. The attached sales report indicates a 10% increase over sales for the same period last year—you can all be proud.
>
> We have to address a difficult challenge. Our marketing budget for the next quarter has been cut by 25%. We need to come up with ideas to achieve the same—or better results—with fewer expenditures. Please come to next week's meeting ready to brainstorm ways we can do that.
>
> Jennifer

It's not clear whether Jennifer wrote that e-mail to tell her team members how pleased she is with their performance or to encourage them to come up with ideas for saving money. She probably wanted to do both. But the two messages end up almost canceling each other out.

Too often, e-mail writing is reflexive writing. Webster's *New Collegiate Dictionary* defines "reflexive" as "characterized by habitual and unthinking behavior."[3] In other words, we write out of habit, without thinking about *why* we are writing.

You'll find that e-mail is a more effective communication tool when you know exactly what you want to accomplish by writing. For example, do you want to . . .

- Answer or ask a question?
- Verify information?
- Send someone a document?
- Promote a good idea?
- Make your opinion known?
- Defend your point of view?
- Justify a request?
- Give advice?
- Convince someone to take action?
- Sell something?
- Ask for help?
- Thank someone or show your appreciation?

Of course, many messages have more than one purpose. But we've discovered that our writing is far more clear—and gets better results—when we focus on *one* primary purpose. That purpose can take one of two forms: to *influence* readers to do something, or to *inform* them about something.

Let's look at each type of purpose separately.

WRITING TO INFLUENCE. You write to influence when your primary purpose is to ask, convince, or persuade a reader *to do* something:

> Send me comments on my proposal by Friday.
>
> Change the procedures for processing invoices.
>
> Give me approval to hire an assistant.
>
> Distribute an agenda at least three days before a meeting.
>
> Reschedule our appointment.

WRITING TO INFORM. On the other hand, your primary purpose might be to give readers information they need to be informed or updated about a subject, to take action, or to make a decision:

> The reorganization team made several key decisions last week. I've summarized them below.

> Computers will be down for three hours on Friday.

> If you want to be reimbursed for your expenses, you need to submit original receipts.

> We plan to launch three new products next spring. Please see the attached descriptions for details.

> The Board will select a new CEO at its next meeting. Here's a list of the candidates:

THINK ABOUT . . .

When an e-mail is clearly written, the writer's purpose is crystal-clear. Here's a quick quiz: What's the writer's purpose for each of the following messages?

Message #1. Purpose?

> Hi, everyone,

> Please send me your agenda items for the quarterly meeting by Friday. I'll draft an agenda and send it back to you for review on March 14. Thanks for your help.

> Tran

Message #2. Purpose?

> Dear Ms. Settles,

> Based on the information you gave me when we spoke last week, we estimate that the cost of building your new Web site will be approximately $7500 and the job will take about four weeks.

I've attached a detailed proposal that includes a working process and a breakdown of the costs. Of course, we'll be glad to answer any questions you might have. We look forward to the opportunity to work with you.

Best wishes,
Arlin Margolin

The purpose of message #1 is clearly to ask readers for their agenda items. For message #2, the purpose is to tell the reader what the cost of building the site will be and how long the job will take. The purpose in every e-mail you write should be that easy to identify.

WHAT'S MY READER'S POINT OF VIEW?

Communication is a two-way process. It takes place only when the message you send has been received *and understood* by *each individual* at the other end. The most common reason for failing to communicate clearly is not stopping to think about the audience—not bothering to look at the message from the *reader's* point of view.

Thinking about your audience helps you in several ways. It's easier to decide what information to include. You're more likely to use the right tone. And you'll get your point across more quickly and in a more focused way.

Considering the reader's point of view begins with these kinds of questions:

- What's your relationship with the reader? Do you know one another, and if so, how well? Are you teammates or colleagues within the same organization? Colleagues from different organizations? Is the reader your manager? A client or a prospective client?

- Is your reader expecting this message? Is this the first message on this subject, or is it part of an ongoing exchange?

- How much does the reader already know about this subject? Does the reader have enough background information or technical knowledge to understand what you're about to convey?

- Is the reader likely to use the information to take action? Make a decision? Be informed?

- What's the reader's interest in this subject? Concerns about the subject? How important is the information to the reader? What issues might the message raise?

- How is the reader likely to feel about this message? Might any part of the e-mail come as a surprise? Be unwelcome news? Be upsetting? Put the reader in a difficult position?

CONSIDER STYLE PREFERENCES

When you think about your readers' points of view, also consider their style preferences. For example, your boss might prefer getting information in well-organized bullet points or another abbreviated format, while one of your clients might be picky about complete, grammatically correct sentences.

Writing to Multiple Readers

If you are writing to someone you know well who is already familiar with the subject, the questions above are usually easy to answer. But what if you have several readers, with differing levels of knowledge, differing needs, and differing concerns?

When sending the same message to several people or to a large group, ask yourself this key question: In terms of this topic, are the readers' needs, interests, and concerns similar enough so that you can send them all the same message? If not, you'll get better results by adapting the message to meet differing needs.

For example:

- Do some people need more background information than others? You might summarize the main points at the beginning of the e-mail, then put the background information below the message or in an attachment. Be sure to tell readers where to find it.

- Do some people have less technical knowledge than others? You might send those readers a plain-English version of the technical information you send your more technical audience.

• Is your purpose to inform certain readers and influence others? In that case, you might get better results by crafting a different message for each group.

Writing to People You Don't Know

What if this is the first e-mail to someone you've never communicated with before? When you know little or nothing about a reader, think about what you *do* know. You can usually make certain kinds of assumptions, based on such factors as the type of organization a person works for, the person's job or position, and the person's relationship to you and your organization. Those assumptions will help you target your message so you get better results.

For example, if your reader is . . .

• A customer service representative: you can assume that he's interested in what you have to say and wants to be helpful (after all, that's his job), knows a lot about the subject but little or nothing about your specific question or complaint, and receives hundreds of similar messages every week.

• A prospective client who has asked for information about your products: you can assume she knows something about your business but needs details that will help her decide whether the products meet her needs.

• A manager in another area who has asked for information about a project: you can assume that the person is interested (she asked for the information), probably needs a summary of key points rather than every little detail, and might not be as technically knowledgeable about the subject as you are.

> **LEARN MORE ABOUT YOUR AUDIENCE**
>
> When what you're writing is very important and you don't know the recipient(s), it can be helpful to learn more about your audience. Talk to people who know your readers, do an Internet search, or make a preliminary telephone call to get the information you need to send a focused

THINK ABOUT . . .

Have you ever received an e-mail on a technical subject you knew little or nothing about? What did the writer do that helped or hindered your understanding?

WHAT'S THE MOST IMPORTANT MESSAGE?

> Hello, Peter,
>
> Your request for information about last year's payments was passed to me from Josh Feldman who is my counterpart in the Denver office. I conducted research into our records in an attempt to locate the payments that you said were missing. We are in the process of transitioning to a new computerized payments system, which is the reason that my research took so much time. According to our records, your company was paid a total of $2585.00 last year for consulting services. $260.00 of that $2585.00 was on check #182394 which was cut on January 7 and the remainder of $2325.00 was on check #211367, which our records show was cut on May 6. We show no other payments made by us to you during the course of the year. We do not know why there is a discrepancy between your records and ours. I hope this information is helpful. As you requested, I have asked Violet Meersham to send you a 1099 this week. Let me know if I can be of any further assistance.
>
> Sincerely,
> Leslie K.

What's the point of that e-mail? It's pretty hard to find. Peter wouldn't have to work so hard if Leslie had gotten right to the point and organized the information differently, as in this revision:

> Hello, Peter,
>
> As you requested, I have asked Violet Meersham to send you a 1099 this week.
>
> According to our records, your company was paid a total of $2585 last year for consulting services. $260 was on check #182394, cut on January 7, and $2325 was on check #211367, cut on May 6. We show no other payments.
>
> I hope this information is helpful. Please let me know if you have more questions.
>
> Sincerely,
> Leslie Karposki

How Do People Read E-Mail?

Think about how you read an e-mail message. Do you sit back with a cup of coffee and ponder every word? Probably not. Instead, you're likely to read only the first few lines before deciding whether the e-mail merits any more of your time. If it does, you'll scan the rest of the message to pick out the important points.

To make sure the most important information gets across quickly and clearly, put your main point—the most important message—at the beginning. Then follow with the facts and ideas that support or expand on the main point, leaving the reader with a complete, coherent message that accomplishes its purpose.

How to Identify the Most Important Message

Before you can put your main point at the beginning, you need to know what it is. Here's a tip: jot down a statement of no more than three sentences that expresses your main point concisely. Then use that statement—perhaps with a few words of introduction to set the context and tone—to begin your e-mail message.

Below and on the following pages are some questions that can help you identify your most important message:

Do you need to ask someone a question? What's the question?

> When can I expect to receive the specifications for the new system?

> How long will it take to get preliminary cost estimates for the redesign?

> Can your team meet with me while I'm in town next Thursday?

THE JOURNALISTIC TRIANGLE

Have you ever noticed that the first paragraph of a newspaper article contains the most important information? The rest of the article provides details that support, explain, expand on, or illustrate that information.

Newspaper editors know that people often scan only the headline and first part of an article. They also know that the final paragraph or two might need to be chopped off to save space. That's why they answer their readers' most important question right at the beginning.

Keep this triangle in mind when you write. Putting the most important information first gets the main point across right away and gives readers a context for the details that are to come.

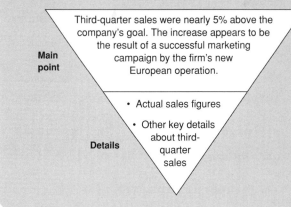

Are you sending someone a document? What are you sending and why?

As you asked, I am sending the report of our investigation as an attachment.

For your information, attached is the preliminary agenda for next month's sales conference. Please let me know by April 6 if you have additions or corrections.

The attached proposal describes details of the health care plan we can provide your employees, including costs.

HOW TO CLARIFY YOUR MAIN POINT

Here's an easy way to figure out what your main point is: Imagine that your reader is about to go through airport security on her way to an important meeting. You have 15 seconds to shout out your message before she disappears into the crowd. What would you say?

Do you want to get buy-in for an idea or a course of action? What is the idea or course of action? What is the key benefit?

Our marketing group has concluded that we could raise our prices by 10% without losing sales.

The task force recommends that we include a gym in the design of the new site.

If you agree to add four weeks to the project timetable, we can take advantage of seasonal discounts for workout equipment.

Do you want to make your opinion known? What is your opinion?

I believe we'd be better off postponing the decision about where to relocate until we know more about the county's redevelopment plan.

After much consideration, it seems to me that it would not be cost-effective to reduce staff at this time.

Your design for the cover of the annual report looks great!

Do you want to justify a request? What are you asking for, and why should your reader say yes?

To meet the deadline stipulated in the contract, we need to hire two temporary programmers immediately.

Would you be willing to meet me for coffee on Wednesday or Thursday of next week? I'd like to learn more about how you started such a successful business.

Because we are a nonprofit institution, we'd like you to consider giving us a discount on your interactive learning series.

Do you want to give advice? What is the advice, and what's the key reason the reader should listen to you?

> I suggest you reconsider leasing the office you told me about yesterday. I once had an office on that street, and it was very difficult for my clients to park.

> Because the position requires so much writing, I recommend that you evaluate each candidate's writing skills before making a hiring decision.

> If you still plan to volunteer as Annual Fund co-chair, you might want to speak with last year's chairperson to find out how much of your time the job is likely to require.

Do you want to sell something? What do you want to sell and what's the key reason the reader should buy it?

> Our retirement planning advisors can help you ensure that your hard-earned money will be there when you need it. We specialize in working with university faculty like you.

> The next generation of our project planning software has a unique feature that allows team members to be more productive by communicating with each other in real time.

> Our experience facilitating nonprofit mergers can help you avoid many of the problems that result when two organizations join together.

Do you want to thank someone or show appreciation? What are you thanking the person for?

> Thank you for letting me know that our proposal will be reviewed by the end of next week.

> Our team was very impressed with the highly informative—and entertaining—presentation you gave at our last regional meeting.

> On behalf of the company, I want to thank everyone in the accounting department for getting the numbers in ahead of schedule.

If Necessary, Introduce the Main Point

Your main point should always come at the beginning of your e-mail. But sometimes you need a few words (never more than a brief sentence or two) to introduce it.

In the examples below, the introductory statement is in regular type, and the main point is in italics:

> The deadline we agreed on is coming up fast. When can I expect the project report?

> It was nice to see you at last week's meeting. Your suggestion that we have a fund-raising event next April sounds great to me.

THINK ABOUT . . .

Think of something you need to communicate by e-mail. Imagine that you have only 15 seconds to get your most important message across. What would it be?

WHAT DOES MY READER NEED TO KNOW?

I'm so tired of reading e-mail messages that go on and on. Why do people think that I need to know everything they know? Just give me the information I need, and then stop. Please!

– MICHELLE BLACK
BCS LEARNING AND KNOWLEDGE
IBM CONSULTING

Last week, I actually missed an important deadline because a colleague left crucial information out of an e-mail. He gave me lots of information—much more than I needed—and still left out the answer to my question. When used incorrectly, even the most efficient form of communication becomes inefficient.

– KATIE WINTER, SENIOR MANAGER
PR & PUBLICITY, MERVYN'S LLC

How often do you stop and think about *exactly* what information a reader needs? Most of us do that only for very important messages. As a result, many of our e-mail messages include unnecessary information or omit important information—or both.

That's because we tend to focus on the information we want our readers to have instead of on the information they need. But if you look at what you write from your *reader's* point of view, you'll see that for an e-mail to be useful, the information it contains should answer all the reader's questions—and *only* those questions.

It can be tricky to figure out what those questions are. Unless you're writing to answer specific questions a reader has asked, you need to think carefully about what the reader's questions are likely to be.

Here's an example: Suppose Gary wants to recommend that his manager, Margo, hold a brown-bag lunch meeting for team leaders once a month.

Margo's question is likely to be, "Why should we hold a monthly brown-bag lunch?"

Gary might come up with these answers:

- Keep everyone up to date on projects
- Let people know what's coming
- Share ideas

The *main point* and the *answers to the question* create a content outline that makes it easy to write a clear, concise message. Notice that Gary added only a few transitional words and a closing to the content outline to come up with this e-mail:

> Margo,
>
> I'd like to suggest that we hold a brown-bag lunch meeting for team leaders once a month. That way, we could keep everyone up to date on the status of our projects and let people know what's coming down the pipeline. These meetings would also give us opportunities to share ideas for solving problems.
>
> Let me know what you think.
>
> Gary

READ CAREFULLY BEFORE RESPONDING

When you're responding to an e-mail, read the entire message carefully to make sure that you fully understand the sender's questions and what information the sender needs. If there are several messages—an e-mail "thread" or conversation—read them all. Otherwise, you might respond to only one question when several have been asked.

Writing to Influence: *Why* Should Readers Do What You Want Them to Do?

In the example above, Gary wanted to influence Margo to do something. Her primary question would be: *Why* should she hold monthly brown-bag meetings?

When you write primarily to influence readers to do something, the content you'll include comes from the answers to that one question, "*Why* should we / I do it?"

 — *Why* should we hire your firm to design our Web site?
 — *Why* should I approve your budget request?
 — *Why* should the customer service team attend communication skills training?

The answers to the question "*Why* . . ." give you the content for your e-mail.

Here's another example of a content outline for an e-mail to influence the reader:

Main point	I believe we should postpone the decision about where to relocate until we know more about the county's redevelopment plan.
Question	Why should we postpone the decision?
Answers	— New area in west part of county might be rezoned — County might offer incentives for building in redevelopment area

On the next page is the e-mail that resulted from that content outline. Once again, notice that the writer added only a few words—an opening, some transitions, and a closing—to expand the outline into a clear, concise message.

Dear Lisa,

After much consideration, I believe we should postpone the decision about where to relocate until we know more about the county's redevelopment plan.

One of the three plans under consideration includes rezoning an area in the west part of the county. That plan includes incentives for building in the redevelopment area.

You can see the text of the proposed plans at www.aspencounty.gov\redev. Please let me know if you need any more information.

Sincerely,
Adam

Writing to Inform: *What* Do Readers Need to Know?

When you're writing to inform, your readers are likely to have more than one question about the subject or topic of your e-mail message.

Here's an example: Suppose that Sarah wants to tell a prospective consultant, Jeremy, that her team is seriously considering his firm for a project. Sarah's main point is that her management team was impressed with Jeremy's presentation and his firm is one of three finalists for the XYZ project.

To decide what content to include in this message, Sarah thinks about what questions Jeremy is likely to have. She comes up with these questions:

- *What information in our presentation was of most use to you?*
- *Is there any other information you need from us?*
- *When can we expect your decision?*

Here are the answers Sarah comes up with to complete her content outline:

- *What information in our presentation was of most use to you?* Your experience with projects like ours and the ways you handled problems.
- *Is there any other information you need from us?* Bios of proposed subcontractors.
- *When can we expect your decision?* Within 2 weeks.

Now that she knows what main point she wants to convey and what information Jeremy is likely to need, Sarah is ready to write the e-mail:

> Dear Jeremy,
>
> Our management team was very impressed with the highly informative—and entertaining—presentation you gave at our regional meeting. I'm pleased to tell you that your firm is one of three finalists for the XYZ project.
>
> The factors that weigh heavily in your favor are your experience with projects like ours and the ways you handled the problems that came up during those projects.
>
> Before we make our final decision, we need one more thing from you: biographical information about your proposed subcontractors. We hope to make a decision within two weeks.
>
> Regards,
> Sarah

THINK ABOUT . . .

Did the people who wrote the last few e-mail messages you received answer all your important questions? Did they include any information that you really didn't need?

WHAT'S THE BEST WAY TO ORGANIZE THE INFORMATION?

In a well-written e-mail, there's a logical order to the information. The main point is at the beginning, and all the other points relate clearly to that main point. Readers never have to skip around to figure out what you're trying to say.

If you've given some thought to your purpose, your audience, your main point, and the questions the reader is likely to have, the most logical order usually makes itself known. But when you have trouble organizing the information, consider the following:

DID YOU JUMP RIGHT INTO THE WRITING WITHOUT THINKING ABOUT YOUR PURPOSE, AUDIENCE, MAIN POINT, AND THE QUESTIONS YOU'RE TRYING TO ANSWER? If so, you're multitasking, trying to organize the information while you're still thinking about what to say. The result could be a confusing e-mail.

DID YOU ADD ANY "EXTRA" INFORMATION? Even when we've thought carefully about what we want to say, most of us tend to put everything but the kitchen sink in our messages—as if everything we have to say will be interesting to our readers. Stick to the point: all the information in the body of the e-mail should support, explain, or expand on the most important message. If something doesn't, leave it out.

HAVE YOU SHIFTED DIRECTION IN MIDSTREAM? Sometimes we start out writing to ask someone to do something, and suddenly we skip to an entirely different topic. Shifting direction in the middle will confuse your reader. It will probably confuse you, too.

ARE YOU TRYING TO PRESENT TOO MUCH INFORMATION? If what you're writing is too complex, use your word processing program to write a separate document and send it as an attachment, using an e-mail message as a cover letter.

DO YOU HAVE SEVERAL UNRELATED MESSAGES TO CONVEY OR ARE YOU WRITING TO MULTIPLE READERS WITH DIFFERENT NEEDS? The result could be a long, rambling message that makes it difficult for any of the readers to find what they need. Think about whether it would be better to write several shorter messages, each focused on one topic or main point, each directed at one reader or group. If you want or need to send all the information in one message, summarize or list the main points at the beginning and then use headings to help readers quickly find specific details.

WRITE OUT YOUR MESSAGE

If you've followed the suggestions in this chapter, writing a clear, concise message will be as easy as pouring a cup of coffee.

When you write the e-mail, do the following:

- For sensitive, complex or high-stakes situations, consider again whether e-mail is really the best way to communicate the information. If it is, use your word-processing program to draft the message. That way, you won't risk sending it before you're ready—you can review and edit it first.

- Use clear, concise, active, specific language that helps get your message across as quickly and accurately as possible. (For more on language, see Chapter Four.)

- Be sure to put your main point—the most important message—at the beginning. If necessary, include a few words or a brief sentence or two that establishes the context. For example, if you're responding to a question, you might restate or summarize the question before launching into the main point: "You asked how much more it would cost to complete the job a week earlier. We estimate the cost to be . . . ."

- If you find yourself adding a lot of extra information, stop and think the situation through again. You might not have adequately considered what information the reader needs.

- If you're struggling to find the right words to express yourself, stop. Take another look at your audience and what you want to say. You might be trying to communicate a mixed message, or you might not have clarified your purpose. Work out the problem before you continue writing.

USE E-MAIL TEMPLATES

My job requires that I write the same six or eight e-mail messages over and over. There are always minor changes, but the purpose and content are essentially the same. To save myself time, I copied each type of message into a file I call "form letters." Now I just select the right message, make the necessary changes, and send it off.

— KATHY BROWN, SALES REPRESENTATIVE
SHERIDAN BOOKS

Form letters, or templates, were invented for a reason. When used properly, they can be real time-savers. A template provides the basic wording and structure; you need only modify the content to fit the specific situation.

Here are what some simple templates look like:

> Dear [name],
>
> Thank you for meeting with me to discuss ways in which our [name of product] can increase the efficiency of your [specific operations].
>
> I've attached a price list that includes a standard installation. As I mentioned, we would be glad to provide detailed costs for customizing our [name of product] to meet your company's specific needs.
>
> Please let me know if you have questions. Otherwise, I'll get in touch with you in two weeks to see what decision you have made.
>
> Regards,
> Jocelyn Yamamoto

~

> Hi, Sales Team,
>
> This is a reminder of the monthly meeting: [date, time, and location].
>
> I've attached a preliminary agenda. Please send me any additions or corrections at least four days before the meeting. Also, please let me know if you will be unable to attend.
>
> Thanks,
> Brenda

~

> To the Events Coordinator:
>
> My group is looking for a site to hold a two-day training program on [dates]. If your facility is available on those dates, please provide information on the following:
>
> [requirements]
>
> If you have questions, please send me an e-mail or call me at the number below. We would appreciate your response by [date].
>
> Sincerely,
> Marietta Brown
> 713-922-7046, ext. 303

Situations like these lend themselves to templates:

- Meeting announcements, agendas, and minutes
- Common requests and responses to common questions
- Regular status reports and project updates
- Sales letters and other marketing messages
- Problem reports
- Trip reports

Guidelines for Using Templates

When using templates, consider the following:

> **SOFTWARE SHORTCUTS**
>
> There are tools available to help you write e-mail messages that you send repeatedly. For example, programs such as Macro Express let you create automated responses or quickly insert prewritten text into messages. You can find many such tools on the Web.

- Instead of starting out to create a template file, let the file "evolve" by adding basic messages as you become aware that you are sending essentially the same message over and over again.

- Keep your template file up-to-date by deleting messages that you no longer need and revising messages when things change.

- Use a template *only* if fits the situation—it can take more time to revise an inappropriate template than to write from scratch.

- Carefully proofread messages written from templates to make sure you haven't inadvertently included old or irrelevant information, used other people's names, forgotten to change dates, and so on.

THINK ABOUT . . .

Do you use templates? How well are they working? If you aren't using templates, how could you use them to streamline the writing process?

E-MAIL AND HAND-HELD DEVICES

More people are reading and writing their e-mail while on the move, using mobile hand-held devices such as BlackBerries or cell phones instead of computers. There are lots of advantages to being able to read and write e-mail from anywhere without having to open a laptop and find a wireless signal. But using hand-held devices for e-mail also creates some problems. Let's look at some of the advantages and drawbacks.

Advantages

When we interviewed people about their use of hand-held devices for e-mail, here's what they mentioned as some of the benefits:

- A quick, easy way to get back to people with answers to questions, suggestions for resolving a problem, or a request

- Keeps messages from building up while you're traveling or on vacation, so there are fewer to deal with when you get back

- Can send a quick e-mail instead of making a phone call, especially when there is inappropriate or obtrusive background noise

Drawbacks

The people we surveyed also mentioned several problems with the use of hand-held devices:

- Faster responses to messages has raised the expectations for a speedy response

- Constant accessibility has raised the expectation of being constantly accessible

- Increased reliance on e-mail instead of person-to-person communication

- More temptation to check e-mail compulsively instead of being "present" and enjoying sights, sounds, and people

- Temptation to read and write e-mail in "down" time—or while driving (not safe!)

- Difficult to write on a small keyboard

- Difficult to read long, complicated messages on a small screen—and messages may be incomplete

- Difficult or impossible to view attachments

- Lowered the bar even further for e-mail with poor grammar and poor spelling

Tips For Using E-Mail With Hand-Held Devices

Here are some ways for making the most productive use of hand-held devices for e-mail:

- *Keep messages short.* When sending e-mail that might be read on a hand-held device, keep messages short and to the point, and put the key information at the beginning.

- *Reduce the need for lengthy responses.* Try to structure messages so recipients either do not need to respond or can answer in a few words. For example, ask questions that can be answered "yes" or "no." If you need a lengthy response, your recipients might decide to wait until they get to a computer—and then forget.

- *Limit messages to one topic.* If you need to change topics, send another message.

- *Make sure it's important enough to send an e-mail right away.* If you're away from your computer, consider whether it would be more efficient—and effective—to make a phone call or wait until you're back at your desk.

- *Describe attachments.* When sending e-mail to people on the move, always describe attachments (briefly) because they might not be able to see them right away. (In fact, it's always a good idea to describe attachments.)

- *Visualize your message on a computer screen.* When sending messages from a hand-held device, remember that recipients are likely to read your messages on their computer, not on another hand-held: What will your message look like with all those abbreviations? With poor grammar, punctuation, and spelling?

- *Turn it off!* To keep e-mail from engulfing your life, resist the urge constantly to check your hand-held for new messages or send messages that don't need to be sent. Give yourself breaks from the network by turning your hand-held device off.

INSTANT MESSAGING

Instant messaging is electronic communication that happens in real time. If you think of e-mail as an electronic form of a letter or memo that needs to be delivered, you can think of

IM as a conversation, like meeting at the water cooler or stopping by someone's office for a chat. Just as everyone involved in a phone call needs to be on the phone at the same time, everyone involved in an IM "conversation" needs to be on line at the same time. Like e-mail, the record of an IM conversation can be saved (and often is). IM conversations can be carried out on a computer or a mobile device.

Tips for Using IM

IM technology is changing rapidly. But no matter how sophisticated the technology, it will always be important to keep the following in mind:

- *Keep it professional.* Instant messages tend to be casual—writers often use incomplete sentences, abbreviate words, and use symbols to convey information. That's usually okay, as long as the message gets across. But this kind of text messaging language is open to misunderstandings and confusion. The casual IM language you use with your friends might not be appropriate in a business setting.

- *Keep it brief.* IM is best for quick back-and-forth exchanges—"Can you take a call at 3 p.m.?" "Who's coming to Thursday's meeting?" "Did you hear from the client about our proposal?"—not for lengthy explanations or solving problems. Once your messages exceed 10–15 words or you've gone back and forth more than two or three times, pick up the phone.

- *Sign off when you don't want to be available.* An advantage of IM is that people can quickly see whether or not you're available to "chat." Be sure to change your IM status when you aren't available. Otherwise, you're likely to be interrupted or distracted by messages popping up on your screen. Also, when your status shows that you're available, people will expect an immediate response.

- *Don't consider IM secure.* No matter what you hear about encryption and security, you can't consider IM a secure form of communication, especially when you are using it to communicate with people outside of your organization. Just as with e-mail, be careful not to use IM to convey confidential or sensitive information,

> **REMEMBER MARK FOLEY?**
>
> In October 2006, Congressman Mark Foley was forced to resign his seat after the disclosure of instant messages he had sent to former White House pages. Always remember that anything you write in an e-mail or an IM could become public.

harass someone, tell off-color jokes, or say anything that someone else might find offensive. And watch your tone. Flippant conversation is flippant conversation, whether it's on the phone, in the hall, or in an electronic message.

> A colleague tells us that he sometimes uses IM for sidebar conversations during conference calls—participants can use IM to remind the person leading the call about a topic to raise or offer answers to questions that come up during the call.

APPLY WHAT YOU'VE LEARNED

1. Print out five e-mail messages you've received recently and answer these questions for each e-mail:

   • Was the main point clear and at the beginning?

   • Was any important information missing?

   • Did the e-mail include any information you didn't need?

2. Print out ten e-mail messages you've sent. For each e-mail, do the following:

   • Write the purpose in the margin. Was it primarily to inform or to influence? Do you think your purpose was clear to your reader(s)?

   • Find the most important message and underline it. Where does that main point come—at the beginning? In the middle? At the end? Is it missing?

   • Consider the subject: Was it appropriate for e-mail? If not, why not?

3. Think of an e-mail you need to write. Develop a content outline for your message by thinking about:

   Your readers. List several points to keep in mind about your reader(s), based on what you know or the assumptions you can make from what you do know.

   _____

   _____

   _____

   _____

   _____

   _____

Your purpose. What do you want to achieve? Is your purpose to pass on information the reader needs or to influence the reader to do something? What action(s) do you want the reader to take?

_____

_____

_____

_____

Your main point. What's your most important message? What would you say if you had only 15 seconds to get that message across?

_____

_____

_____

_____

The reader's most likely questions. What question or questions does this e-mail need to answer? List those questions, and then answer them.

_____

_____

_____

_____

_____

_____

4. Think of the messages you need to communicate repeatedly with only minor changes: meeting announcements, sales letters, answers to common questions, and so on.

- Choose at least two of those messages. Think about the kinds of changes that need to be made for different audiences and situations.

- Develop a template for each message that will let you quickly insert details to customize the message for specific readers and situations.

- Create a folder or folder for the templates so you can find them quickly when you need them. (See Chapter 3 for more on creating and using folders.)

NOTES

NOTES

2

LAUNCHING YOUR MESSAGE

Everyone says e-mail's so easy. But back in the good old days, all I had to do was compose a memo or letter, print it out, and stick it in an envelope. Now I have to worry about things like attachments, what to put on the subject line, whether to use color or bullets, when it's okay to forward a message I get . . . writing's actually more complicated than it was before.

— LESLIE FRIEDMAN, EDITOR

That writer put into words a common frustration with e-mail communication: even though it can save us a lot of time and work (and trees), it raises lots of issues.

Here are some common questions:

- How do I make sure my message makes sense? Conveys the right tone?

- How can I format my e-mail message so it's easy to read?

- Do I always have to use a salutation? A closing?

- Do I always have to write in complete sentences?

- Does my punctuation and grammar have to be perfect?

- When and how should I send attachments?

- What should be on the subject line?

- How and when should I address the e-mail?

These questions and the many others that come up as we use e-mail don't have quick and easy answers. But the tips and techniques on the following pages will help you send e-mail that achieves your goals and meets the needs of your readers.

READ FOR SENSE

If you followed the guidelines in Chapter One, your message probably makes sense. Just to be sure, read it through. Look at the message from your *reader's* point of view. If you were the reader, would it make sense to you?

Make any necessary changes to the content of the message right away, before worrying about the formatting, writing the subject line, or entering the address. If there's any unnecessary information, delete it. If there's anything essential you forgot to mention, add it.

Be careful, however: if you find yourself rewriting the message, moving things around, or adding a lot of new information, stop. Take another look at your purpose, your audience, your main point, and the questions the e-mail needs to answer.

CHECK THE TONE

When you read for sense, also check the tone. What kind of attitude does the e-mail convey? Is it too abrupt? Too casual? Too formal? Not friendly enough?

Once you're satisfied that your message is clear, you can easily adjust the tone by adding, deleting, or changing specific words, as shown in these examples:

Abrupt	Get me the revisions by Thursday.
Polite	Please be sure to get me the revisions by Thursday.
Polite	I would appreciate your getting me the revisions by Thursday.
Casual	Got a lot on my plate right now—not sure I can take on a new gig.
Professional	I'm very busy at the moment, and I'm not sure I can take on a new project.

Formal   Prior to July 23, payments can be sent only through the Postal
Service. Subsequent to that date, payments can be made electronically via our Web site.

Friendly   Before July 23, you can make payments only by mail. After July
23, you can make payments on our Web site.

Don't Use All Caps or All Lowercase Letters

Text written in all caps (ALL CAPS) conveys an abrupt and demanding tone even when the
words and subject are relatively tame:

> IF YOU WANT TO ATTEND THE MARCH MEETING, WE NEED
> YOUR REGISTRATION FORM BY FEBRUARY 15.

You might use all caps occasionally to emphasize a word or two, but even then, the tone can
be somewhat abrupt:

> If you want to attend the March meeting, we need your
> REGISTRATION FORM by FEBRUARY 15.

Using all lowercase letters doesn't convey an abrupt or demanding tone, but it's not
professional, and it gives the impression that you don't consider the message very important:

> if you want to attend the march meeting, we need your registration
> form by february 15.

An entire e-mail written in all lowercase letters can also be hard to read.

THINK ABOUT . . .

Can you recall receiving an e-mail that had what seemed to be an abrupt,
demanding, or rude tone? One that seemed too casual for the situation? How
did the tone make you feel about the message and the person who sent it?

MAKE THE E-MAIL EASY TO READ

How easily can you follow this e-mail message?

> Hi, Laura,
>
> The total contribution you've made for this tax year is $7200. The maximum contribution for the year is $11,000 plus an additional $1000 if you are age fifty or older. If Craig wishes to contribute the maximum, he can contribute $4800 for the rest of the year (12,000 less 7200 = 4800). If he can get the Salary Reduction Agreement form to me by Tuesday we can take advantage of the last three months in this tax year (4800 divided by 3 = $1600). Next year's maximum is $12,000 plus an additional $2,000 if age fifty or older. Our tax year begins with the December pay period (the check that's issued on January 1.) I hope this information is helpful.
>
> Best wishes,
> Pierre

Pierre clearly didn't think about how that message would look on a computer screen—or on a hand-held device. Even though it's well written, it takes a special effort to understand it.

Notice how much easier the message is to read when it's broken down into short paragraphs, with a blank line between each paragraph:

> Hi, Laura,
>
> The total contribution you've made for this tax year is $7,200. The maximum contribution for the year is $11,000, plus an additional $1,000 if you are age 50 or older.
>
> If Craig wishes to contribute the maximum, he can contribute $4,800 for the rest of the year ($12,000 less $7,200 = $4,800). If he can get the Salary Reduction Agreement form to me by Tuesday, we can take advantage of the last three months in this tax year ($4,800 divided by 3 = $1,600).
>
> Next year's maximum is $12,000 plus an additional $2,000 if you are age 50 or older. Our tax year begins with the December pay period (the check that's issued on January 1).
>
> I hope this information is helpful.
>
> Best wishes,
> Pierre

Remember what we said in Chapter One about the way people scan e-mail messages instead of reading them word for word? If a message is clearly written and presented, scanning it quickly should be enough for the reader to grasp the important information. That's our goal as writers: to help readers understand our messages as quickly, easily, and accurately as possible.

Keep these points in mind:

- Short sentences and paragraphs are easier to read than long ones.

- Lists are easier to read than sentences and paragraphs.

- Information is easier to follow when there's space between list items and paragraphs.

- Symbols such as bullets, boldface, and icons might not show up on other people's computers the way they do on yours.

CAN A PARAGRAPH BE ONLY ONE SENTENCE LONG?

Sure it can. One-sentence paragraphs are fine in e-mail messages, as long as the sentence communicates a complete thought.

> Mark,
>
> As you asked, I'll make the necessary changes to the project time-table and send you a revised calendar by next Friday.
>
> Deanna
>
> ~
>
> Marketing Team,
>
> We've scheduled the telephone meeting for 10:30 a.m. tomorrow, May 3.
>
> Billy

> **TELL A STORY**
>
> Notice how easy it is to tell a story, with beginning, middle, and end, in three sentences.
>
> The system was down from 6:13 p.m. to 11:27 p.m. last night. The technicians traced the problem to a broken connection at the LYCX junction. Repairs were made, and all similar connections will be checked before the end of the week.

Use Short Sentences

There is little agreement among writing experts about how long a sentence should be. As a general rule, we think that e-mail messages are more readable when sentences stay within an average of 15–20 words, with one primary thought per sentence. Keep your sentences even shorter when you're conveying complex ideas or technical information, writing to people whose primary language is not English, or writing messages you suspect will be read on hand-held devices. In Chapter Four, you'll find suggestions for staying within these guidelines.

Use Short Paragraphs

Most of us get lost when there are no breaks in a large block of text, especially when we're reading from a screen. Help readers follow your points by keeping paragraphs to a maximum of three sentences and focusing each paragraph on one key fact or idea. Also, make sure that each sentence in a paragraph is related to the main point—don't shift the focus or begin a new topic in the middle.

Use Lists

When I need to send an important message to a client, I present it in a way that the reader can easily digest. For example, I give a quick overview of the content at the beginning, and then I organize the details into bullet points.

— MARNIE AULABAUGH, CO-FLOUNDER
FRESHBAIT, A CREATIVE COMPANY

Bulleted lists offer an easy way to communicate your message quickly and clearly. They also save you valuable time by simplifying the writing process.

Lists help you and your reader by . . .

- Getting information across more quickly and in fewer words

- Separating key points, details, or items of information

- Focusing the reader's attention on specific information

- When appropriate, serving as checklists—for example, when you are presenting readers with items on which they need to take action

- Reducing the chance of grammar and punctuation errors

Guidelines for Using Lists

Following are some actions you can take to use lists effectively:

KEEP LISTS SHORT. All the list items should be visible on one screen, so readers don't have to scroll. If you have lots of information to convey, put it in an attachment.

INTRODUCE THE LIST. Every list needs an introductory statement, if only a few words, that tells readers what the list is about:

> Summary of project status:
>
> *   The client has approved the design
> *   We are on schedule and within the budget for Phase One
> *   We need to hire three more programmers for Phase Two

KEEP THE LIST PARALLEL IN FORM. All the items on the list should be presented in the same form so readers can grasp the relationship between items. For example, if one item begins with an "ing" verb, all the items should begin with "ing" verbs. If one item begins with a noun or a noun phrase, all the items should begin the same way. If one item is a complete sentence, each item should be at least one complete sentence; similarly, if one item is a fragment, each item should be a fragment.

Not parallel

Here are the agenda items for Friday's meeting:

- Discussion of the new health plan. The plan will be available to all full-time employees.
- Whether to revise the procedures manual
- Early retirement policy

Parallel

Here are the agenda items for Friday's meeting:

- Discussion of the new health plan that will be available to all full-time employees
- Decision about whether to revise the procedures manual
- Formulation of an early retirement policy

Not parallel

We need the following to finish the proposal:

* Final cost estimates—to come from Sam
* Patrice is responsible for the list of subcontractors
* Waiting for project plan which Franco is drafting

Parallel

We need the following to finish the proposal:

* Final cost estimates—to come from Sam
* List of subcontractors—to come from Patrice
* Project plan—to come from Franco

MAKE SURE ALL THE ITEMS BELONG ON THE LIST. In other words, every item must be directly related to the introductory statement. An unrelated item, such as the last item in the list below, can be confusing:

Please review the attached directory listing for the following:

- Any errors in the biographical information
- Up-to-date e-mail addresses
- Accuracy of the telephone and fax numbers
- Send your corrections to Ilariya Marsh no later than the end of next week

USING MINI-PARAGRAPHS IN LISTS

It's often appropriate for list items to be mini-paragraphs (three sentences or less):

> Here is a summary of our findings:
>
> - The McNear's site is large enough for us, but it is more than 10 miles from the freeway and 12 from the ferry. We would have to provide shuttle service for staff who commute by bus or ferry.
>
> - Both the Parker Valley and Talley Road sites are located near transportation hubs. Parker Valley, however, is too small to house everyone in one building. Talley Road, while large enough, needs substantial renovation.
>
> - The White Oaks building complex meets all of our requirements—close to transportation, large enough, in need of little renovation, etc. However, it is 25% more expensive than any of the alternatives. We might be able to negotiate a lower price for a longer lease.

To fix that list, pull out the last item and use it in the opening or as a closing statement:

> Please review the attached directory listing and send your corrections to Ilariya Marsh no later than the end of next week. Look for the following:
>
> - Any errors in the biographical information
> - Up-to-date e-mail addresses
> - Accuracy of the telephone and fax numbers

USE WHITE SPACE.   Always leave a space between the introductory statement and the first list item. Also, if any item in the list is more than one line long on the screen, leave space between each item so the reader can easily see where one item ends and the next begins.

No space needed between items (although you can include one if you wish):

> I've attached the following:
>
> • Budget figures for the next quarter
> • Draft of the job description for the new position

Space needed between items:

> The team made two important decisions at yesterday's meeting:
>
> • During the next six months, job responsibilities will be rotated among all team members so that everyone will be cross-trained
>
> • People will have the option of starting their shifts at 7 a.m. and leaving at 4 p.m.

BE CONSISTENT WITH INITIAL CAPITALIZATION AND END PUNCTUATION. List items that are fragments of sentences do not have to begin with capital letters (unless the first word is a proper name). But if you capitalize the first word of one item, capitalize the first word in every item.

When list items are a single sentence or less in length, you don't need a period. The period is not wrong, but it's not necessary. If you use a period at the end of one item in a list, however, use it at the end of all the items in that list.

You never need a semicolon at the end of an item in a list. (See Chapter Four for more on semicolons.)

FRAGMENTS OR FULL SENTENCES?

It's okay to use fragments in lists. A list allows you to convey complete thoughts without writing complete sentences. That's because the opening statement is actually part of every item in the list.

> Below are three features that customers who responded to the survey said they would like:
>
> – access to a 24-hour help line
> – e-mail statements
> – a longer grace period for payments

THINK ABOUT . . .

Do you use lists when you write e-mail? Do your lists follow the guidelines we discussed above?

SALUTATIONS

I know e-mail is different from formal correspondence, but is a salutation needed at the beginning? Some messages are addressed like letters, with "Dear Ms. Sher," and sometimes it's "Hi, Julie." Some people just start out with the message. How do you know what's right?

— JULIE SHER
HEALTH CARE CONSULTANT

E-mail doesn't always need to follow the same rules as formal business correspondence. But a salutation or greeting is like saying "Hi" or "Hello" when you begin a conversation. It helps you . . .

- Establish a personal contact by using the reader's name

- Assure readers that the e-mail is meant for them

- Set the tone

Salutations or greetings can be formal or informal, depending on the situation. Any of the following would be fine:

Dear Mr. Wolinsky,	Hi, Bob,
Dear Bob,	Hello, Bob,
Bob,	

If you're writing to a group, you can begin with . . .

Dear Clients,	To My Clients:
Hi, Team,	Hi, Everyone,
Hello, Associates	

Sometimes all you need is "Hi" or "Hello."

> **COMMAS IN SALUTATIONS?**
>
> These days, people often omit the comma between the "Hi" or "Hello" and the person's name for informal salutations:
>
> Hi Bob,
> Hi, Bob,
>
> We like the comma. But unless your organization gives you specific guidance on this issue, you can use it or leave it out. Either form is okay. Be sure, however, to use the comma after the person's name. It's not okay to leave that one out.

Guidelines for Salutations

Your company policy might include guidelines for determining which kind of salutation to use. Otherwise, you can use the ones that follow. (See Chapter Five for more on developing an e-mail policy.)

ARE YOU WRITING TO SOMEONE INSIDE OR OUTSIDE YOUR ORGANIZATION? You usually need a formal salutation ("Dear . . .") only for people outside the organization. But there are exceptions. If you're writing to someone who is senior to you, such as a director or chairman of the board, it might be more appropriate to use "Dear Ms. Moreno" or "Dear Director" instead of "Hi, Allison."

ARE YOU WRITING TO A COLLEAGUE OR FRIEND? Use an informal salutation or greeting, or just begin with the person's name.

HAVE YOU MET OR COMMUNICATED WITH THE PERSON BEFORE? It's sometimes better to use a formal salutation when you write to someone you've never met, spoken with on the phone, or communicated with by e-mail.

DID THE PERSON USE A FORMAL SALUTATION WHEN ADDRESSING YOU? When replying to an e-mail message, note the way the person addressed you. If the person used a formal salutation, you'll probably want to use a formal salutation in return.

ARE YOU WRITING TO SOMEONE IN ANOTHER COUNTRY? Unless you already know the person, you might want to use a formal salutation, at least when you first begin to exchange messages. People outside the United States tend to be more formal in business settings.

> **COLONS IN SALUTATIONS?**
>
> A common question is whether to use a colon after a formal salutation, the way you would if you were writing a business letter.
>
> Dear Mr. O'Connor:
>
> The evolving style is to use a comma instead of a colon.
>
> Dear Mr. O'Connor,
>
> Unless your organization's style guide addresses this topic, do what feels right to you.

> **DO I ALWAYS HAVE TO USE A SALUTATION OR GREETING?**
>
> When people ask this question, we say, "Not always, but usually." You can leave the salutation off when you are holding an extended back-and-forth e-mail "conversation" and sometimes when you are providing a brief answer to a question. But an e-mail that begins without so much as "Hi" can seem abrupt. It never hurts to be polite and friendly.

THINK ABOUT . . .

Do you ever receive e-mail that has no salutation or greeting? Under what circumstances does that seem okay?

What kind of salutation or greeting do you normally use when you send e-mail messages? How do you make that decision?

CLOSINGS AND SIGNATURES

Is it no longer the practice to finish up with "Yours Truly," or some ending like that? Lots of the e-mail I get sort of drops off—no closing, no signature, no company name, no address, not even a telephone number in case I need to reach the person who sent it. Sometimes I can't tell whether I've reached the end of the message or something just got left out.

— GAIL SCHECHTER, PH.D.
PRESIDENT, BIOINTELLIGENCE

When I get an e-mail from someone who is asking me to do something, especially with a tight deadline, a simple "Thanks" in the closing can make a big difference. I notice that the closing can impact my interpretation of the message. If it's friendly (but not flowery), it leaves me with a positive feeling.

— MICHAELA HAYES, SENIOR MANAGER
LA PIANA ASSOCIATES, INC.

Good manners and efficiency dictate that every e-mail message include a closing that lets readers know they've reached the end of the message and a signature that tells them, at the very least, how to reach you.

Closings

A closing is like the period that ends a sentence—it lets the reader know you're done. Like the salutation, the closing can be formal, informal, or casual.

Formal	Sincerely, Regards, Yours truly
Less formal	Best wishes, Warm regards, Thank you
Casual	Thanks, See you soon

To extend the tone you established with the salutation, it's a good idea to choose a salutation and a closing that complement one another.

For brief messages to friends and colleagues, it's sometimes okay to close with only your name or even your initials. But keep in mind that this kind of closing can have a rather abrupt tone:

Parker,

UPS picked up the package today. It should arrive by next Tuesday.

Sheila

$\sim$

Thanks for the update, Brendon—will let you know if I need more details.

J.

Signatures

It's very frustrating to get an e-mail without a phone number that tells me how to reach the person. That can really cause problems when we're dealing with important information and time is of the essence.

—JASON TANG, PROJECT MANAGER

An e-mail without a signature is like a voice mail message without a name or telephone number: the assumption is that the other person knows who you are and how to reach you. But just as someone you call might not recognize your voice or have your phone number handy, a recipient might not recognize your e-mail address or know to reach you by phone.

As a courtesy to recipients and to help avoid problems, always include at least your name and telephone number. It doesn't hurt to include your e-mail address, even though it's on the FROM line in the header. Including your e-mail address in the body of the message makes it easier for people to find you if they're not replying immediately. And if you use more than one e-mail address, make sure that the e-mail address on the FROM line is the one you want people to use.

Depending on the situation and your organization's policy, also include all or some of these details:

- Your title or position
- Your company name
- A fax number
- A mailing address
- The URL for your Web site

WORRIED ABOUT WHETHER YOUR MESSAGE WAS RECEIVED?

Sometimes you don't need a reply to an e-mail, but you do need to know that it was received. You might be able to request an automated delivery receipt, but people often set up their software to prevent the sending of such receipts.

An alternative is to put a line requesting a reply at the beginning or the end of your message, something like, "Please let me know that you got this message." That way, you won't have to waste another e-mail or phone call to find out whether your message ever arrived.

CHOOSE A PROFESSIONAL USER NAME

Clever e-mail handles like "ProfoundThinker@hotmail.com" are fine for communicating with your friends and conducting your personal business. But they're not appropriate for the workplace, and they don't give recipients any clues about who you are.

When people decide which messages to open first, they often ignore e-mail from people they can't quickly identify. And even if recipients recognize your unique user name, people to whom they forward your messages might not. So for business, choose a user name that identifies you and presents a professional image.

Using Signature Files

You might not want to use the same signature for every message. For instance, your formal company signature probably isn't appropriate when you're writing to a friend; conversely, you might not want to give out your home address and phone number when writing to business associates.

Set up your preferences so the signature you use most often is the default—the one that's automatically appended to an e-mail unless you specify otherwise. Then set up a few alternate signatures. For example, if your default signature file is very long—your title or position, mailing address, fax number, etc.— create an abbreviated version for e-mail conversations. It's annoying to see a long signature block repeated over and over again in a series of back-and-forth messages.

Keep the information in your signature files up-to-date with your current phone number, e-mail address, and other important contact information.

THINK ABOUT . . .

How do you usually sign your e-mail messages? Do you include enough information? Too much information? If you use signature files, when was the last time you reviewed them? Do you have alternative signatures for different situations?

PROOFREAD!

In some circles, there's a belief that a professional writing style isn't important for e-mail—that the rules of grammar, punctuation, and spelling don't apply. Let's look closely at that belief. Suppose you received the following message from someone you've never met. What would be your image of the person who wrote it?

> Dear Supplier Partner:
>
> I am pleased to announce: that InfoSearch has adcepted a offer, from Online Libary, Inc.
>
> to purchase it's website. Marcus Wellenby, Onlines CEO and I have work non-stop in recent weeks to put the deal together with minimum affects for both customers and our supplier partners. This will inable the InfoSearch.com website to contine to operate and, give it a chance to realize it's potential.
>
> I want to apologize to any of you who have had a difficulty, in contacting us
>
> while we have operated with a skeletel staff in anticipation of this transatcion. I also want to personnelly thank you. For your support and for a wonderful asociation to those of you I have the pleasure of meeting.
>
> Best Regrds,
> Suzanne Boyles

USE YOUR SPELL-CHECKER—CAUTIOUSLY

It's a good idea to run a spell-checker before sending out an e-mail. But you can't count on it to catch every error. For example, it missed three in this sentence:

> Within the next to months, we plan to implement some change in procedures that will effect the customer service and billing departments.

Because you're smarter than the spell-checker, you probably saw that the words "to," "change," and "effect" were misspelled. Here's a corrected sentence:

> Within the next **two** months, we plan to implement some **changes** in procedures that will **affect** the customer service and billing departments.

Your spell-checker won't catch errors like those because it looks only for misspelled words. In this example, the words were spelled correctly—they were just the wrong words.

Chances are, you wouldn't take Suzanne's message very seriously. After all, how credible is someone who can't take the time—or doesn't know how—to write a message without glaring errors?

We think error-free e-mail is so important that we've devoted a large part of Chapter Four to such issues as using correct grammar and punctuation. For now, we'd like you to remember two key points:

- The e-mail you write conveys a particular image to your readers. If your grammar, punctuation, and spelling are sloppy, that's the image you'll convey.

- Certain errors—such as misplaced modifiers, awkwardly constructed sentences, fragments that fail to convey complete thoughts, and incorrectly used punctuation marks—can mislead readers or make it difficult for them to understand what you're trying to say.

Before sending out an e-mail message, do yourself and your readers a favor by proofreading it. Proofreading doesn't take long, and it can go a long way towards promoting a positive, professional image of you and your organization.

SENDING ATTACHMENTS

E-mail lets us use attachments to share documents of all sizes and types quickly and easily with people all over the world. You create the attachment as a word processing document, a spreadsheet, a presentation, or in another format, then simply append it to an e-mail. As long as the recipients have compatible software, they can open, save, print out, and edit the attachment as if they had created it themselves. They can also forward it to others.

But the ability to send and receive attachments comes with its own set of hazards. Has any of the following happened to you?

- The cover letter says there is an attachment, but it's not there
- There's an attachment that's not mentioned in the cover letter
- The cover letter says there's an attachment but doesn't tell you what it is or what you're supposed to do with it—Comment on it? Forward it? File it?
- You go to the trouble of opening an attachment you don't need
- You receive an attachment your software can't read
- An attachment takes too long to download
- An attached file takes up too much space on your computer
- An attachment transmits a virus to your computer

What Attachment?

> Marlon,
>
> Thanks for reminding me about the meeting—I'd completely forgotten.
> Did you mean to send the agenda? It wasn't attached. Send again?
>
> Thanks,
> Lily

Marlon did something most of us have done—he forgot to attach the attachment. Lily had to ask for it, and then Marlon had to send out another message, which meant extra time and work for both of them.

It's easy to avoid this common problem: make it a
habit to attach the file *before* composing the message. Then, if you're originating the message,
check again to make sure the attachment is
attached before entering the recipient's address; if
you're replying to an e-mail, the address will
already be on the TO line, so double-check
before sending to make sure you've included the
attachment.

**MAKE SURE TO ATTACH THE
RIGHT FILE**

If you're selecting a file from a list,
it's a good idea to double-check to
make sure you've attached the right
file. It's all too easy to select the file
above or below the one you want.

Oops—Did I Miss the Attachment?

Always tell your readers that there's an attachment. Otherwise, they might delete, forward,
or save the message before noticing that something has been attached.

Why Am I Getting This?

It takes time to open and read an attachment. Save your readers time by telling them what it
is instead of forcing them to open it just to find out.

Think carefully about whether all the recipients, especially those on the CC and BCC lines,
actually need the information. If only your primary reader—the person (or people) named
on the TO line—needs the attachment, you might want to send a separate e-mail, without
the attachment, to the others.

When you forward an e-mail that came with an attachment, think about whether or not to
include the attachment. And when you reply to a message that came with an attachment, be
sure to remove it if your system doesn't remove it automatically. After all, the person you're
replying to already has it.

What Am I Supposed to Do With This?

Unless you know the recipient is expecting the attachment, include a cover e-mail that clearly
explains what you expect the reader to do with it.

> Here are three designs for your new brochure. We'd like to know by Monday which design you prefer.
>
> I've attached the draft of the project report. Please use the "track changes" feature to comment. After I receive everyone's comments, I'll produce a final draft.
>
> The quarterly budget has been revised again. (It's attached.) Can you forward it to all your managers? They can contact me directly if they have questions.

Also, if the attachment is long and complex, consider summarizing it briefly in the body of the e-mail message.

What Language is This, Anyhow?

When communicating with people outside your organization, you can't assume that their computer's software is compatible with yours. For example, your word processing program might be the most recent release, which your recipient's older version can't recognize. If you can, check out compatibility. If you think it might be necessary, tell a reader what software and what version was used to create the attachment.

What if you suspect—or know—that a recipient can't open an attachment? You can cut and paste the information into the body of the e-mail, create a PDF file, or post the information on a shared Web site. Or you can send it the old-fashioned way—by mail or fax.

WHY USE A PDF FILE?

There are several advantages to converting a document to a PDF file before sending it out. For one thing, you can make sure the file retains the original formatting. For another, PDF files are not easy for other people to change. Also, there's less chance of transmitting a virus with a PDF file than with other file formats.

Why Is This Taking So Long?

The speed with which people can download attachments varies. It can take a significant amount of time to download even a medium-size file. Graphics and photographs increase the download time substantially.

One way to send large files is to break them up into smaller files and send them in several messages. Another is to use file-compression software such as WinZip or StuffIt to reduce file size. You can compress one large file, or you can compress several files into one folder. If you use compression software to "zip up" a file, check with your recipients to make sure that they can unzip the file.

How Do I Know Where This Attachment Has Been?

Most computer viruses are transmitted in attachments, so it's not surprising that people have become reluctant to open attachments unless they know and trust the sender. If you're not sure that a recipient is willing to open an attachment, ask before sending it.

Here are some ways to reduce the possibility of unwittingly transmitting a virus in an attachment:

- If a document isn't too long and the way it's formatted isn't important, consider pasting the information into an e-mail message rather than sending it as an attachment

- Scan your outgoing e-mail and attachments with the most up-to-date antivirus software

- Send the document as a PDF file, which is less likely than other file formats to transmit a virus

- Keep your own computer healthy by refusing to open attachments of unknown origin and making sure that your virus-checking software is up to date.

THE SUBJECT LINE

My manager sent me to a seminar on the effective use of e-mail. My number one takeaway was that I needed to craft better subject lines. My messages weren't getting the attention they deserved because people weren't bothering to open them. Now, instead of using subject lines that are vague and unappealing, like "Coffee Sales," I use subject lines that go to the heart of the matter, like "Sales in District 9 up this quarter," and I'm getting better responses.

— JEFF ANGELL
SENIOR DIRECTOR OF MARKETING
ARAMARK CORPORATION

Imagine a newspaper without headlines. How would you know what stories you wanted to read? A well-written subject line is like the headline for a newspaper article: it draws the reader's attention and tells the reader what the e-mail is about. The subject line gives the reader a reason to open the message. It's also your first and most important opportunity to get your message across.

Notice the difference between the original and revised subject lines in the columns below:

Original	Revision
New Program	Accepting applications for flex-time program
Changes	Health benefits to change next year
Proposal	Strategic Planning Project Proposal
Dates	Kickoff Meeting—Apr 2, 6, or 9?

The revised subject lines are informative and compelling. They grab the reader's attention and provide enough information to make the reader want to read the message.

WORD SUBJECT LINES CAREFULLY

Certain words or phrases can get your message sent to the spam, or junk mail, folder, where your reader will probably never see it. Here are a few examples:

For your eyes only	Opportunity Knocks
Profit	Free
Look at this!	Confirmation of order
$$	!!!!

Your organization might have a list of words and phrases to avoid. Check with the people who provide you with technical support.

By the way, always put something in the subject line. A blank subject line is not only useless to the recipient, it might get your message tagged as spam.

WATCH THOSE ! POINTS

In a misguided attempt to call attention to their e-mail messages, some writers "liven up" their subject lines with language and punctuation that makes the message seem more important than it is.

> Only 3 days left to apply!

> Your presence required!!

Not only can anything with an exclamation point get your message sent to the spam folder, it's unfair to mislead readers by conveying a false sense of urgency. Remember the boy who cried "Wolf!" If you do it too often, no one will ever take you seriously. If a message really is urgent, your system might let you flag it or mark it in some way. Better yet, make a phone call to let the recipient know it's coming and needs immediate attention.

How to Write a Useful Subject Line

We recommend these strategies for writing subject lines that really work:

MAKE THEM DESCRIPTIVE. An engaging subject line includes enough information to pique the reader's interest. The best subject lines both summarize and introduce the contents of the e-mail.

Not descriptive	Budget
Descriptive	Marketing budget increased 10%

MAKE THEM SPECIFIC. An effective subject line includes enough detail to distinguish it from similar e-mails. An appropriate subject line not only tells readers what the e-mail is about, but it lets recipients find the e-mail again by searching for a key word or phrase.

Vague	Report
Specific	Robotix Computer Upgrade Project Report

PUTTING THE ENTIRE MESSAGE IN THE SUBJECT LINE

A quick way to convey very brief messages is to put the whole message in the subject line, followed by a symbol such as ## or EOM to indicate that the message is ended:

Confirming lunch 5/27 at 12:30, your place ##

Agenda for June 6 meeting now on Web site EOM

MAKE THEM CONCISE AND CLEAR. A compelling subject line gets the message across without unnecessary words or obscure abbreviations.

Wordy and confusing	This msg inclds the details abt nu mktg pln
Concise and clear	New marketing plan details

CHANGE THE SUBJECT LINE WHEN THE SUBJECT CHANGES. When replying to or forwarding a message, and when you're engaged in a back-and-forth e-mail "conversation," pay special attention to the subject line. If the focus remains on the original topic, you might not need to change it. But neglecting to change the subject line when the topic changes can mislead or confuse the reader.

CONSIDER THE LENGTH. Long subject lines are often truncated, especially when people read e-mail on hand-held devices. If you can't avoid a long subject line, make sure the key information appears in the first few words so it will show up even if the end of the line gets cut off.

THINK ABOUT . . .

How much attention do you pay to the subject line? Do you usually stop to consider whether the subject line accurately describes and previews the message? Can you think of a time that you forgot to change the subject line when you replied to a message but changed the topic?

LAST BUT NOT LEAST: ADDRESS THE MESSAGE

My friend, who does all her business via e-mail, gave me a really useful tip: "You know how the pilot checks all the instruments before the plane takes off? Do that with your e-mail. Before you put in the address, do a final check—reread the message; make sure the subject line's okay, the attachments are attached, and you've included the right salutation, closing, and signature block; and run spell-checker." What good advice! It's kept me from sending a few messages that had serious problems.

— JEAN E. SCHORE
SCHORE MARKETING ASSOCIATES

Addressing e-mail is pretty straightforward, right? Unfortunately, it's not. There are several questions to consider if you want to make sure that a message goes to the right people:

- Do you have all the recipients' correct, current e-mail addresses?

- Are you originating, replying to, or forwarding a message?

- Are you writing to one person or many?

- Do you want someone to receive a copy without the other recipients' knowledge?

It's relatively easy to address a message that you're originating and sending to only one individual: simply put that person's e-mail address on the TO line. It's also easy when you're replying to a message without sending copies to anyone else: click "Reply," and the recipient's address automatically appears on the TO line.

But many of the messages you send require some thought. Here are examples of decisions you might need to make:

- You receive a message from a client about a project that is over budget. The addresses on the CC line indicate that the client sent copies to five people in her office. Do you reply only to the client or to everyone who received the original message? Do you edit the CC line so your reply goes only to selected individuals? Do you use the BCC line to send a blind copy of your reply to your own manager?

- You get a message from the CEO asking you to identify issues that you and your team would like to see addressed at the management team's strategic planning retreat. You plan to forward this message to your staff. Should you forward it as is? Should you add your own comments? Do you want to add specific messages for selected individuals?

- You're sending a survey to everyone in your organization asking whether people are interested in working at home for a couple of days a week. You want each person's reply to come only to you, not to everyone on the distribution list. How can you make sure that you are the only recipient of the survey responses?

It's worth taking the time to decide how to answer questions like those. A misdirected message can be annoying—and it can have serious consequences.

Who Should Get This Message?

E-mail makes it pretty easy to send copies everyone on the planet. The result, as we all know, is a huge amount of unnecessary mail. Wouldn't it be better if writers took even a fraction of a second to think about who actually needed the e-mail message they were about to send?

To decide whether specific people need to receive a specific message, ask:

- Do they have the answers to the questions you're asking?
- Have they asked for the information you're sending?
- Do they need to know that you want or need something done?
- Will they make a decision or take action, based on the information you're sending?
- Is there a reason that they should be kept in the loop—informed about what's going on?

The last question is the one you'll really need to ponder. Does anyone other than the members of your team need the minutes from the last meeting? Does your manager need—or want—the entire series of messages that you and your client exchanged about the project budget? Does everyone need to know about changes in the health plan, or only those who will be affected?

We all need to take responsibility for making sure that the right people—and only those people—get the messages we send. We need to:

- Have a good reason for sending someone a message or a copy of a message

- Regularly review and cull our distribution lists

- Take a last careful look at our designated recipients before hitting Send

---

USING AN ADDRESS BOOK

An electronic address book can be a real time-saver—as long as it's up-to-date. When you get an e-mail from someone you'll be corresponding with again, add the person to your address book right away. When someone sends you an address change, make the change immedi-

---

THE POWER OF PERSONALIZATION

I get hundreds of e-mail messages every day. The ones that I am most likely to read and respond to are those that are personalized. Instead of writing to the "Marketing Managers," sometimes a colleague will take the extra minute to send a separate e-mail to each of us, using our names in the salutation and adapting the content a little. That makes a big difference.

– Katie Winter, Senior Manager
PR & Publicity, Mervyn's LLC

Guidelines for Addressing E-Mail

To save yourself and your recipients time, do the following when you address an e-mail message:

PAY ATTENTION WHEN ENTERING ADDRESSES. When you're originating an e-mail, make sure you have all the recipients' current addresses and type them in correctly. Otherwise, the message might be bounced back as "undeliverable."

> **DELETE UNNECESSARY OR INAPPROPRIATE CONTENT**
>
> When using the "Reply to all" option, forwarding a message, or sending a copy of your reply to someone else, delete any portions of the original message that the recipients do not need—or should not receive.

DISTINGUISH BETWEEN THE "REPLY" AND "REPLY TO ALL" OPTIONS. "Reply" sends your message only to the person who sent it to you. "Reply to all" sends your message to that person *and* anyone whose address is listed on the CC line.

View the "Reply to all" option with a wary eye. Do all the people who received the original message really need copies of your reply? Any of them? Can you let the sender of the original e-mail decide whether to forward your reply to specific people? Delete from the TO and CC lines the addresses of everyone who doesn't need—or should not receive—your reply.

THINK VERY CAREFULLY BEFORE FORWARDING OR SENDING COPIES OF A MESSAGE. Ask yourself: Is this information private or confidential? Is this an appropriate message for others to see? Do others really need to receive this e-mail? Do they need all the information? Will I waste their time by sending it to them? Do they need an explanatory comment or additional information?

EDIT YOUR DISTRIBUTION LISTS REGULARLY. Add new addresses when necessary and remove the addresses of people who no longer need to be on a specific list. That way, the right people, and only the right people, receive the messages you send.

CREATE DIFFERENT DISTRIBUTION LISTS FOR DIFFERENT SITUATIONS. Instead of sending everything to everyone, create distribution lists that fit the various situations in which you need to send e-mail to groups. For example, perhaps everyone on your team needs the summary of what takes place at management meetings, but only the people who plan to attend need the meeting agenda.

USE THE BCC LINE WITH CAUTION. BCC means "blind carbon copy." When you put an address on the BCC line, that person receives a copy of the e-mail without the knowledge of any of the other recipients. Sending a blind carbon copy isn't always appropriate—it's like allowing someone to listen secretly in on a telephone conversation—so think carefully before using that option. Think especially carefully before sending a BCC to someone's boss.

CONSIDER USING "BCC" WHEN SENDING E-MAIL TO GROUPS

The BCC line is most useful when sending a message to a group without revealing all the recipients' e-mail addresses and taking up lots of space in the message header. Address the e-mail to yourself and enter the recipients' addresses on the BCC line. Everyone will get the message with your name on both the TO and FROM lines.

You might need to warn people that group e-mail will come that way so they don't think the message is a mistake or spam. Also, the BCC technique doesn't work with all systems, so do a test run before sending out your mailing.

When you use BCC for the e-mail you send to a group, people can reply only to you, not to the entire group. That restriction can be useful. But if everyone in the group needs to see a reply, you'll have to forward it.

THINK ABOUT . . .

How many e-mail messages did you receive this week that you didn't need? How much time did it take to deal with them?

When was the last time you updated your distribution lists?

During the past week, did you send e-mail to anyone who didn't need it?

APPLY WHAT YOU'VE LEARNED

1. Check the salutations on ten recent e-mail messages you've sent and received. Are they appropriate to the situation? Too formal? Too casual? Too abrupt? How would you change them? Write three of the original salutations or greetings on the lines below. Then write the changes you'd make.

   Original   *Revision*

   _____   _____

   _____   _____

   _____   _____

2. Look at five recent e-mail messages you've sent and five you've received. Do they have useful closings and signatures? What changes would have helped?

   _____

   _____

   _____

   _____

   _____

3. Do you already have a signature file that automatically adds a signature block to your e-mail? Do you have at least one alternative signature? If so, review those files to see whether they need any changes.

   If you don't have a signature file, create at least two that would be appropriate for the different kinds of e-mail you send. Decide which signature file should be your default—the one that will be added automatically to every message unless you manually select a different one.

   If you don't know how to create a signature file, consult your Help menu or the people in your organization who provide technical support.

4. Go through a newspaper or magazine. Circle some headlines that draw your attention. Notice how the headline writer gave you a little preview of the article in those few words. Write the best three headlines below.

_____

_____

_____

_____

5. Look at the subject lines from five e-mail messages you've sent and five you've received. Do they meet the criteria of a well-written subject line discussed in this chapter? If not, how could you revise them so they would be more effective? Write three of the original subject lines and their revisions below.

Original _____

_____

Revision _____

_____

Original _____

_____

Revision _____

_____

Original _____

_____

Revision _____

_____

6. Write effective subject lines based on these scenarios:

Simon needs someone to volunteer to provide administrative assistance for the Heart Association project.

Subject line _____

_____

Melissa can't attend the Verizon meeting on February 6 but wants someone to attend in her place and take notes.

Subject line _____

_____

Grisha's opinion is that the draft of the Clorox presentation needs a lot more work.

Subject line _____

_____

7. Do you regularly send e-mail to groups? Review the distribution list for at least one of those groups. Add or remove addresses to make sure that the right people—and only the right people—get those messages.

NOTES

3   MANAGING YOUR E-MAIL

We isolated a group of e-mailers, about 20 percent of all work e-mailers, we called "power users." Most power users manage their e-mail better than average users, they value their e-mail more highly, they use their e-mail in many more ways, and they are more likely to say that e-mail saves them time. But even among power users, there are hopeless cases, those who let their e-mail pile up, untended, in their inboxes.

— DEBORAH FALLOWS, SENIOR RESEARCH FELLOW
PEW INTERNET AND AMERICAN LIFE PROJECT

Most of us would agree that e-mail has made enormous changes in the way we work. Whether it makes us more productive is still an open question. Reading, responding to, and managing e-mail can consume vast amounts of our valuable time, and we don't always use that time as well as we could. In fact, more than 70 per cent of the e-mail users we surveyed in 2006 thought that they could use their e-mail time more productively.

Even those of us who approach our work systematically tend to approach e-mail in a completely unstructured way. We check incoming messages too often. We interrupt other activities to open new mail as soon as it arrives. We ignore the increasing volume of mail in our inbox, promising ourselves to take care of it "one of these days." We do things in the wrong order, waste time responding when no response is needed, and lose important messages in folders we never bother to clean out, like overstuffed cabinets crammed with junk we can't seem to organize or throw away.

Managing your e-mail isn't difficult, but it does take some thought and attention. In this chapter, you'll find a tool kit of tips that will help you manage your e-mail, instead of letting it manage you.

QUICK QUIZ

Which statements are true for you?

☐ I check my e-mail more often than I need to

☐ There are currently 50 or more messages in my inbox

☐ Some of the messages in my inbox are more than four weeks old

☐ I have trouble finding messages that I need to see again

☐ I often check my e-mail while talking on the phone

☐ I feel as if I should read and respond to every message as soon as it comes in

☐ I dread opening my inbox after being away from the office for even a few days

☐ I get lots of messages I don't need

☐ Messages I send often get bounced back as "undeliverable"

☐ I have trouble deciding which messages to keep and which to delete

If you checked any of those items, the information in this chapter will help you manage your e-mail more efficiently.

REDUCE E-MAIL INTERRUPTIONS

A study commissioned by Hewlett-Packard has found that excessive day-to-day use of technology . . . can be more distracting and harmful to the IQ than smoking marijuana. . . . The research found that 62 percent of adults are addicted to checking e-mail and text messages. Half of the workers would "respond to an e-mail immediately or within 60 minutes." One in five is "happy to interrupt a business or social meeting to respond to an e-mail or telephone message." . . . The IQ decline was the equivalent of missing a whole night's sleep.

— BENJAMIN PIMENTEL, "E-MAIL ADDLES THE MIND"
SAN FRANCISCO CHRONICLE, MAY 4, 2005

I'm pretty good about not letting phone calls or people interrupt me while I work on something that requires concentration. I've learned to let my voice mail take a message and to put a sign on my office door that lets people know when I will be available. But e-mail—I can't seem to resist that little "ding" that tells me a new message has landed in my inbox. No matter what I'm doing, I stop to see what it is.

— MELISSA LUKIN
EXECUTIVE DIRECTOR, CORA

Recently I met with a financial advisor who wants my business. While we were meeting, his computer kept signaling that a new message had dropped into his inbox. Each time, he glanced over at the computer. It was just a moment—he didn't actually open the messages—but I was annoyed by the way that his attention shifted away from our discussion. It made me wonder how much attention he'd give to my investments.

— GLORIA PARETSKY
INDEPENDENT INVESTOR

Each new e-mail is like a little gift that seems to cry, "Open me!" What could it be? The response to my budget increase request? A query from a prospective client? Confirmation of my conference application? Acceptance of my article for publication? Kudos from my manager for a job well done?

Incoming e-mail can easily distract you from the task at hand. Checking and responding to every message as it drops into your inbox is almost a reflex, like picking up the phone every time it rings, even when you are busy with something else. It's no wonder that by the end of the day, many of us feel as if we've accomplished very little.

In a recent article in the *Harvard Business Review,* Dr. Edward M. Hallowell called this phenomenon Attention Deficit Trait (ADT). He described the afflicted worker as one who is unable to stay focused on a single work-related task. ADT, unlike the neurological disorder, Attention Deficit Disorder (ADD), is caused entirely by environmental factors—including being constantly bombarded by e-mail at work.

To combat ADT, Dr. Hallowell recommends, among other things, that you set up specific times to check your e-mail. He also suggests that you begin your day by starting and completing one or two important tasks before allowing yourself to "get sucked into vortices of e-mail or voice mail."[4]

Tips for Controlling Your E-Mail Habit

The way you use e-mail in your work dictates how often you need to check your inbox. If you suspect that you're checking e-mail obsessively, and if e-mail is interrupting your work, use the following methods to control your habit:

FIRST, TURN OFF YOUR COMPUTER'S "YOU'VE GOT MAIL" SIGNAL. Do it right away. You will have taken one giant step toward removing yourself from temptation. If you don't know how to turn off the e-mail alert, consult your Help menu or the people in your organization who provide technical support.

UNLESS YOU'RE EXPECTING SOMETHING IMPORTANT, CHECK YOUR E-MAIL ONLY AT CERTAIN TIMES. Even if you're expecting an urgent message, try to check while you are between other activities, not in the middle of them. And when you scan your message list to see whether that urgent e-mail has finally arrived, avoid the temptation to open other new messages.

INSTEAD OF RESPONDING TO EVERY MESSAGE AS YOU READ IT, "CLUSTER" YOUR RESPONSES. For example, if one person has sent several messages, read them all, combine your responses into one succinct message, and write a new subject line. You'll save yourself time, and the recipient will be thankful.

DON'T CHECK E-MAIL WHILE YOU'RE TALKING ON THE PHONE. Checking e-mail while you're on hold is one thing; reading and responding to e-mail while you're in the middle of a conversation is another. If you give less than your full attention to each activity, they'll both suffer.

NEVER CHECK E-MAIL IN THE MIDDLE OF A MEETING. It's distracting when people stop paying attention to what's going on in a meeting to check their e-mail. It's also rude. Even if you're meeting with only one or two people, wait until you're done to check your e-mail.

IF YOU NEED TO CONCENTRATE ON SOMETHING, REMOVE YOURSELF FROM TEMPTATION. In other words, get away from your computer. Take your work into a conference room or library, or go to a café. If you need a computer, borrow a colleague's. Or use your laptop—but don't connect it to the Internet. (And leave your BlackBerry behind.)

FOCUS ON THE E-MAIL YOU'RE WRITING. When you're crafting an important e-mail, ignore any new messages that appear in your message list. You can look at them when you're done.

DON'T CHECK E-MAIL JUST BECAUSE YOU'RE BORED. Checking e-mail should be a purposeful activity. If a break is what you need, take a break. Get up from your desk. Get some coffee. Take a walk.

Reduce the Amount of E-Mail You Receive

We all like to get mail. But too much e-mail can take over your day. Here's how you can reduce the volume of mail that comes into your inbox:

ASK TO BE TAKEN OFF DISTRIBUTION LISTS FOR INFORMATION YOU DON'T NEED. Get yourself off lists for teams you no longer belong to and newsletters you no longer want. When you check your inbox, drop any messages from those senders into a folder for unwanted items. Then schedule time at least once a week to go through that folder and send messages as needed to remove your name from those lists. (See Page page 87 for more on using folders.)

ASK PEOPLE TO COMBINE THEIR MESSAGES. Do some of your frequent correspondents tend to send a new e-mail whenever they happen to think of a new idea, have a question, or want to share a bit of information? Tactfully ask if they wouldn't mind combining related items into one message instead of sending lots of little messages.

USE THE PHONE FOR DISCUSSIONS. E-mail is great for passing on information and asking questions. But it's usually more productive to discuss something over the phone than in a steady stream of back-and-forth e-mail messages. Use e-mail to arrange a time for the telephone meeting.

DIRECT E-MAIL NEWSLETTERS AND OTHER INFORMATIONAL MESSAGES TO A SEPARATE FOLDER. Most e-mail software will let you specify that messages from certain senders automatically land in a separate folder, not in your inbox. That way, they won't clutter up your inbox, and you can read them at your leisure.

SET UP SEPARATE MAILBOXES FOR CERTAIN MAIL. When you expect a high volume of e-mail on a specific topic or during a specific period of time, set up a separate mailbox, with a separate e-mail address, just for that mail. For example, if you've sent out a job posting, set up a new mailbox and put that address on the posting.

MANAGE—AND COMMUNICATE—EXPECTATIONS. Let your coworkers know how often you plan to check your e-mail and within what time frame they can expect you to respond. If you set up clear guidelines and follow them, your colleagues will respect your decision to focus on one thing at a time.

THINK ABOUT . . .

What changes can you make right away to manage e-mail interruptions and reduce the amount of mail that comes into your regular inbox?

RESPONDING TO MESSAGES

Everyone has a horror story about hitting "reply" and sending the wrong message to the wrong person. That happened to me when I was part of a marketing project team. I got a message from the team leader saying that I only had two days left to finish the market research. I was so irritated by the tone of her e-mail that I forwarded the message to my boyfriend and wrote "she really bugs me" at the top. But instead of hitting "forward," I accidentally hit "reply." I still remember the sinking feeling when I realized what I had done. Of course, I apologized profusely, but the damage was already done.

— NAME WITHHELD BY REQUEST

Most of us don't usually waste our time writing unnecessary letters or making unnecessary phone calls. Yet nearly everyone who uses e-mail sends messages that don't need to be sent. To make matters worse, every message you send is likely to result in at least one message back to you.

Many of the unnecessary e-mail messages we send are responses to messages we receive, so it helps to stop and think before clicking on "reply." Consider the following:

DO YOU NEED TO RESPOND? Many of the messages you receive may need no response. If the sender is only passing along information and has not asked for a reply, reading and then filing or deleting the e-mail is probably enough.

IS E-MAIL APPROPRIATE FOR THIS TOPIC? Think about what we discussed in Chapter One about whether e-mail is appropriate for a message. Those guidelines are just as true for a response. Just because the sender uses e-mail for a sensitive or confidential topic doesn't mean that you have to—or should—use e-mail to reply. It might be better to make a phone call or set up a meeting. Or maybe you don't need to respond at all.

HAS THE MESSAGE MADE YOU FEEL ANGRY OR UPSET? Try not to respond while you're experiencing strong feelings. Give yourself some time to consider what you want to say and how you want to say it. Think about whether you should discuss the matter on the phone or in person. If you do decide to respond via e-mail, use your word processing program to compose your message. Then read it carefully before pasting it into an e-mail.

IS THIS MESSAGE PART OF A BACK-AND-FORTH E-MAIL CONVERSATION? Know when to stop the conversation. For example, it's not always necessary to say "thank you," and certainly not more than once. If you're exchanging e-mail on a specific topic with a group, resist the temptation to add just one more comment—"Great idea!"—or weigh in on every issue—"Fine with me."

> **DELAY SENDING YOUR E-MAIL**
>
> Most e-mail programs, including Outlook, will let you delay the delivery of your messages for a specified time, from a few minutes to a few hours. The message sits in your outbox until the time you've specified, giving you a chance to change your mind. The delay feature is particularly useful if you tend to react emotionally or impulsively to e-mail—it gives you time to cool off and reread your message for tone. To learn how to use this feature, check your Tools and Help menus or ask your technical support people.

IS THIS MESSAGE PART OF A GROUP DISCUSSION? Group discussions sometimes go on and on, continuing long after they've ceased to be productive. When that happens, take the initiative to help the group recognize that the discussion is over. Summarize the key points and next steps. Let everyone know that you think the discussion has achieved its objective, so you can move on to something new.

HAVE SEVERAL PEOPLE SENT MESSAGES ON THE SAME TOPIC? Read all the messages carefully. If necessary, summarize the key points or questions from the individual messages. Then combine your responses into one e-mail that includes answers to questions, asks new questions, and so on.

IS THERE RELEVANT PREVIOUS CORRESPONDENCE? Make sure you've read all the related e-mail before jumping into a dialogue with your own comments. You could irritate the rest of the group if you're not up to speed.

ARE YOU TEMPTED TO FORWARD THE MESSAGE BECAUSE YOU THINK IT'S INTERESTING? Before sending the message on, think carefully about whether the *recipient* is likely to find the information interesting and useful.

THINK ABOUT . . .

How do you usually respond to e-mail messages? Do you often respond when no response is needed? Can you remember a time when you responded in the heat of the moment and wished you had taken time to consider your reply more carefully? How can make sure your responses make good use of your and your recipients' time?

KEEPING YOUR INBOX CLEAN

One strategy some people use with their e-mail is simply to do very little. They just let e-mail sit in their inboxes, figuring if an important message gets lost or forgotten long enough, the sender will either resend the message or call them on the phone for a response. These people are throwing the responsibility of communication back to the sender.

— DEBORAH FALLOWS, SENIOR RESEARCH FELLOW
PEW INTERNET AND AMERICAN LIFE PROJECT

How many messages in your inbox . . .

- Are sitting there unread?

- Are waiting for a reply or action?

- Should have been deleted or filed away weeks ago?

Your inbox should be for active messages, and *only* active messages. If you let messages sit around for days or weeks while you figure out what to do with them, you'll soon experience the disorder known as Inbox Clutter. The symptoms include disorientation, confusion, a feeling of being overwhelmed, headaches, stomach pains, and an almost irresistible urge to throw something large and heavy at the computer screen.

There's only one cure for Inbox Clutter, and the remedy needs to be applied on a regular basis: read *all* your new messages every day, and as soon as you read a message, act decisively—respond to it, forward it, file it, or delete it.

Schedule Your E-Mail Tasks

It's hard to provide general rules about how often to check for new mail, what time or times of day to check, and how much time to allow. E-mail might be peripheral to your business, or it might be the primary way you get your work accomplished. But even those of us who do most of our work via e-mail can make better use of our time by scheduling our e-mail tasks.

Find a schedule that works for you—and stick to it. If you get lots of important mail, you might check your inbox every hour or two; if your e-mail is more routine and doesn't usually require an immediate response, half an hour or so once or twice a day might be enough to handle incoming mail. You might make checking e-mail the first and last tasks of the day, or you might prefer to allot time at the beginning of the day (while you're having coffee), right before lunch (when you're a little hungry), right after lunch (when you're a little sleepy), and at the end of the day (just before you need to meet your carpool or catch a train).

Some people check e-mail as a transitional activity between tasks. For example, they check for new messages between one meeting and the next; when they finish one task and are about to turn to another; or when they've just finished a phone call and are about to start something new. Checking e-mail as a transitional activity can work well if you're careful not to get so caught up in your new mail that you neglect to move on.

LET PEOPLE KNOW WHEN YOU'LL RESPOND

If you're not going to act on a message immediately but you think the sender expects a reply, let him or her know when you will respond:

> I received your questions about the schedule, Jackie. I'll get back to you by the end of next week.
>
> Lillian

THINK ABOUT . . .

Consider the amount of e-mail you receive on a normal day. How urgent are those messages? How often do you need to check your inbox? How much time do you need to allot? What times of day would work best?

Act Decisively

Do the math: if you leave only 10 messages in your inbox every workday, you'll have 50 messages within a week and 200 messages within a month.

— MICHAEL CHUN, DIRECTOR
GLOBAL EQUITY DERIVATIVES, DEUTSCHE BANK

In June, 2004, Internet legal visionary and Stanford Law Professor Lawrence Lessig wrote the following note to the hundreds of people who had sent him e-mail since 2002: "Dear person who sent me a yet-unanswered e-mail, I apologize, but I am declaring e-mail bankruptcy." Dr. Lessig explained that he had spent 80 hours the previous week sorting through more than two years' worth of unanswered e-mail. Realizing that "without extraordinary effort" he would never be able to respond, he acknowledged that he had failed in the most basic form of "cyber decency."

FROM MICHAEL FITZGERALD, "CALL IT THE DEAD E-MAIL OFFICE"
WIRED NEWS, JUNE 7, 2004

Messages can build up with blinding speed if you ignore too many of them or put off making decisions about them. It's tempting to leave messages in your inbox to deal with "later." But somehow "later" never comes, and before you know it, you'll have hundreds of messages beckoning for attention.

Use a Systematic Approach

Your goal whenever you check your inbox should be to *do something with every message:* delete it, respond to it, forward it, print it out, or save it to a folder.

There are several ways to approach your inbox. You can scan it quickly for urgent messages and those that can be deleted immediately, then go through the remaining messages one by one. You can read the messages in sequence, from top to bottom or bottom to top, and deal with them one at a time. Or you can search for messages from specific people or on specific topics. Find or develop a system that works for you—and use it.

Here's a suggested process:

1. If you're waiting for something important, scan the newly arrived messages quickly to see whether it has come in. Take action on that message before looking at any of the others.

> **ABOUT THE SORT FUNCTION**
>
> You can sort the messages in your inbox—or in any of your other folders—in a variety of ways: by sender, subject, file size, whether the e-mail has an attachment, and priority. The sorting options usually appear in a header at the top of the inbox or folder. Sorting is a good way to find a specific message or group of messages quickly. It can also help you take a new look at the messages in your inbox when you don't have time to go through them all.

2. If any new messages are marked urgent, check to see whether they really are—people often mark messages urgent just to get your attention. If they do require immediate attention, take action.

3. Take a first pass through the remaining messages. As you scan them . . .

    *   Delete any you obviously don't need or that obviously require no action ("Will send the report on Friday," or "Office supply sale starts next week!")

    *   Write quick responses to any messages you can reply to in a few words ("I'm glad you're planning to submit a proposal—RFPs will go out on Friday." "February 8 works for me. See you at 1:30." "I'll be glad to talk with you. Call me tomorrow at the number below.") Then delete the message or save it to a folder.

    *   Forward any messages that don't require a response from you but which someone else needs to see, adding a brief comment if necessary ("Here's Kim's idea for a better customer complaint-handling procedure—looks good to me.") Then delete the message or save it to a folder.

    *   If all you need to keep is the sender's address, save it to your address book right away and then delete the message.

4. Take a second pass through the messages that remain. Those are the ones that require more thoughtful action. You might need to do some or all of the following:

- Compose a careful response

- Forward the message to an individual or a carefully selected group, with detailed comments of your own

- Summarize the message or message string and send the summary to an individual or a group

- Print out the message and/or the attachment, then delete, forward, or file the e-mail

- Make a telephone call or schedule a meeting to discuss an issue raised in the message

- Do some research before you answer the sender's questions

> **DON'T OPEN MESSAGES YOU DON'T NEED TO READ**
>
> It's a waste of time to open messages that you clearly don't need to read. You can often tell by the subject line, the sender, or the few words that appear in a preview window that you can simply delete, forward, print out, or file a message without reading it or responding to it.

If you can't handle a message on the spot, schedule time to act on it. With a good reason, you can leave it in your inbox for a day or two, maybe even a week. But remember that messages left in inboxes for more than a week are major contributors to Inbox Clutter.

Reduce the Amount of Mail You Receive

Have you ever returned to your office after an absence to find 500 messages staring at you from your inbox? That's not a pretty sight. To reduce that number:

- Set your system to send an automatic reply that tells people you're out of the office and when you'll return. Although the original e-mail will still land in your inbox, the information that you're away might keep people from sending additional messages.

- Alert regular correspondents that you'll be gone, and ask them not to send you e-mail until a specific date.

- If your location and schedule permits, check your e-mail remotely from time to time and clear out any messages you can handle quickly.

- If you're on vacation or unable to check e-mail while you're away, consider asking an assistant or colleague to check your inbox for messages that can be answered, filed, or deleted without consulting you.

THINK ABOUT . . .

How often do you check your inbox? Too often? Not often enough? Do you check it at the right times of day?

Do you use a system to keep your inbox clear? Does it work well? If not, what changes might you make?

CREATE AN ELECTRONIC FILING SYSTEM

A woman we occasionally work with just can't manage her e-mail electronically, so she prints out every e-mail she gets and puts them in a pile next to her desk. Eventually, the pile gets so big that it falls over. I don't know what she does after the messages have been strewn across the floor.

— ANNIE MARTINEZ, COMPUTER CONSULTANT

Last week, I needed an e-mail I'd gotten from a client with several detailed questions he'd asked about his tax status. I spent more than an hour searching my computer files. Nothing. I ended up having to ask the client to send the information again.

— MARCUS OSTROSKY, CPA

E-mail is a written record of conversations, decisions, and information. But those records are useful only if you can find them. Just as you need a system for storing printed documents so they can be easily retrieved, you need an electronic system for storing e-mail messages.

Every e-mail program gives you the option of setting up folders and subfolders—in other words, of creating an electronic file cabinet—but how you set up and organize those folders is up to you. Think about the best ways to group the messages you keep so that you can find them easily.

Pointers for Using Folders

These suggestions can help you organize your saved e-mail:

SET UP FOLDERS THAT REFLECT THE WORK YOU DO. Create primary folders for broad categories—Projects, Administration, Clients, Marketing—then create subfolders for specific types of messages and topics within each category. Label the folders so you can tell at a glance what's in them.

You can also set up folders that are dated for future action—like a tickler file. When you can't or don't need to act on a message right away, save it to a dated folder. When the date comes up, take action on the messages the folder contains.

> **IS IT OKAY TO SET UP SUBFOLDERS OF MY SUBFOLDERS?**
>
> Sure it is, but be careful. Too many levels of subfolders will make your head spin. Organizing is always good, but over-organizing means extra work: you might not be able to find a document because it's buried in a subfolder of a subfolder of a subfolder. We recommend no more than three levels: primary folder, subfolder, and subfolder of the

DECIDE WHETHER TO SAVE SENT MESSAGES AUTOMATICALLY. The advantage of automatically saving copies of messages you send in a "Sent Messages" folder is that you have a record of what you've written. The disadvantage is that Sent Messages folders quickly become overcrowded. Also, if lots of those messages include large attachments, they'll take up a lot of space on your system.

To avoid that buildup, some people go through their Sent Messages folder once a week or so, delete the messages they no longer need, and move the others to labeled folders. Others turn off the "save sent messages" option for some or all of the messages they send. Still others don't use the "save sent messages" option at all. Instead, they send copies of messages they want to keep to their inbox, then move them to relevant folders.

SET UP NEW FOLDERS AS THE NEED ARISES. If, for example, you find yourself receiving several messages on a new topic and you'll need to refer to them later, set up a new folder for that topic. When you begin a new project or get a new client, set up new folders for those messages.

REDESIGN YOUR FILING SYSTEM WHEN IT NO LONGER FITS YOUR NEEDS. If you change jobs or hand off some of your responsibilities to others, your current system of folders might no longer work. Schedule some time for a redesign.

BE CAREFUL WITH "MISCELLANEOUS" FOLDERS. Although you might need a folder called Miscellaneous or Messages to Keep, use it only for the rare messages you need to keep that do not warrant folders of their own or belong in any that you've already set up. An overcrowded Miscellaneous folder isn't very useful because you're likely to have trouble finding specific messages when you need them.

REVIEW ALL YOUR FOLDERS PERIODICALLY. As folders grow larger, set up subfolders. Delete items you no longer need. If you empty a folder you won't be using again, delete it.

When you clean out an overstuffed folder, sort the messages by date, sender, or subject to find the ones you no longer need. You might look at the older messages first. Or you might search for all the messages related to a client you no longer have or a project that's completed.

> **REVIEW AND EMPTY JUNK MAIL FOLDERS**
>
> Most systems include a spam or junk mail folder that automatically receives messages that are identified as junk. But valid messages can get sent there, too. Review your spam folder often, move messages you need to your inbox, and then empty the folder.

FREE UP SPACE ON YOUR SYSTEM BY ARCHIVING OLD MESSAGES. Use your system's "archive" feature to store old messages you no longer need right at hand but can't delete. Archiving is like moving the files from a file cabinet into a storage box in the basement. They're still accessible if you need them, but they're no longer in your way. If you wish, you can set it up so that all messages older than a certain date are archived automatically.

You can't—and shouldn't—archive everything. Ask yourself how likely you or your organization is to need the message again: Will you need it as a reminder of a conversation or an agreement? As part of an audit trail? To demonstrate compliance with regulations? Is there a chance the message could become evidence in a court action?

Because retaining certain kinds of documents is becoming increasingly important for organizations, yours is likely to have a policy that specifies which documents to archive and how long they are kept.

SAVE E-MAIL IN ANOTHER FORMAT. If you need to work with the information in an e-mail, use your system's Save As feature to save the message as text or in another format. For example, if you need to edit the information or incorporate it into another document, save it as a word processing document. You can also copy all or part of a message to a document.

EDIT MESSAGES BEFORE SAVING THEM. If you need to keep only some of the information from a message, delete the unnecessary content before saving the e-mail to a folder. Most e-mail programs let you do that; if not, you can forward the message to yourself, deleting the parts you don't need. Save the edited message and delete the original.

PERIODICALLY BACK UP YOUR E-MAIL FOLDERS. If the information in an e-mail is important enough to save, you'll want to make sure that it doesn't disappear for good if something happens to your computer.

TAKE OUT THE TRASH. The messages you delete ordinarily go into a "trash" or "deleted items" folder. Be sure to empty that folder from time to time, especially if it contains a lot of messages with large attachments. Trash builds up quickly, and it can slow down your system. (But remember—emptying the trash doesn't delete the messages from your computer—see Chapter 5 for more.)

THINK ABOUT . . .

Have you ever backed up your e-mail folders? Do you know how? What would happen if you lost those messages?

How many items are sitting in your trash folder? When's the last time you emptied it?

APPLY WHAT YOU'VE LEARNED

1. Keep a log to track your e-mail activities for the next five days. Every time you open your e-mail screen, note the following:

   • Time of day

   • What else you're doing (talking on the phone, just finished a meeting, writing a report, ready to go to lunch, etc.)

   • Why you opened your e-mail screen (to check your inbox, send an e-mail, look for an e-mail message you're expecting)

   • How long you spent on the e-mail-related activity

   At the end of the five days, analyze the information in your log and make some decisions about how best to schedule your e-mail activities.

   There's a blank log page at the end of this chapter.

2. Go through your inbox. Try to take action on every message: respond, forward, print out, file, or delete. If you can't act on a message immediately, schedule the time to do so.

3. For the next week, keep a list of all the messages you receive because you are on a distribution list of some kind—newsletters, announcements, special offers, team projects. At the end of the week, take steps to get off the lists you no longer need to be on.

_____

_____

_____

_____

_____

4. If you haven't already done so, set up an electronic filing system with folders and subfolders that represent your work. If you already have a system, review it and redesign it if necessary so that it meets your current needs.

5. Schedule at least an hour during the next two weeks to clean up your e-mail folders by deleting or archiving messages you no longer need.

6. Make a contract with yourself to handle your e-mail more efficiently. List five actions you will take this week and post the list in plain view. Renew your contract every Monday morning for the next six weeks. There's a blank contract page at the end of this chapter.

E-MAIL ACTIVITIES LOG

Keep this log for at least five days. Then assess the way you schedule your e-mail activities and make any changes needed to use your time more productively. (You can download and print a copy of the log from our Web site.)

Start date _____ End date _____

Time of day	Task / activity I've just completed or am engaged in	Reason I opened my e-mail screen	Time on e-mail-related activity

CONTRACT WITH MYSELF #1

WEEK OF _____

To handle my e-mail more efficiently, I will take the following actions this week:

1. _____

_____

_____

2. _____

_____

_____

3. _____

_____

_____

4. _____

_____

_____

5. _____

_____

_____

NOTES

_____

_____

_____

_____

_____

_____

_____

_____

_____

_____

_____

_____

_____

_____

_____

_____

_____

_____

NOTES

4 PRESENT A PROFESSIONAL IMAGE

I was invited to submit a proposal to develop a strategic plan for a local nonprofit. I was swamped with work, but consultants never say no, so I put together a proposal really quickly and attached it to an e-mail to the executive director. A few days later I got a reply telling me that I was not one of the finalists. Actually—and I am ashamed to say this—the director told me that there were multiple mistakes in my e-mail and the attachment and that lack of detail made her concerned that I would not be able to handle all the details in the strategic planning process. I was very embarrassed. I wish I had spent the few extra minutes to proofread what I wrote.

— BELINDA KIM, CONSULTANT

Suppose you received the two e-mail messages that follow from people you'd never met. What would be your image of the writers? Of their organizations?

> FROM: designer43@aol.com
>
> TO: c.reilly@brcm.com
>
> SUBJECT: files
>
> i am sosorry I didnt get these to yu mon or tues, retrieving txt files isnt much trble & I told paul I would do it, they want these files for their archives so, as longas i dont run into any tech probs ican get them 2 u t-day. Cant make RTF files frm Quark finals, can make ASCII txt files, will they do u any good atthis point. ill plan on getting them to u ASAP if u can still use them.
>
> Fredo

FROM: customerservice@Argona.com

TO: Nellie Michaels

SUBJECT: Problem

Your message to Argona about your problem has been recieved and forwarded to me for reply. Please be advised that you are one of our most valuable customers and and we are axious to be of any assistance that we can be. With regard to your e-mail, I am able to offer you the following information. We will be pleased to repair your computer accessory that would involve shipping it to our repair center but prior to shipping the equipment it is necessary that you first speak with a technician in advance. A shipping address cannot be given for our repair centers, however, a case number needs to be created, details about the problem need to be documented in that case. In order to reach a techncian please, consult the instruction manual that was received with your accessory.

I hope you will find this information helpful and that answers all of your questions. Thank you for visiting our site and contacting Argona. Please feel free to contact the undersigned should you have any additional questions.

Sincerley,
Mina

Fredo's message-mail is just plain sloppy, as if he had written it while doing something else. Mina's is wordy, difficult to follow, and filled with errors. Both messages are not only hard to read, they give recipients a poor impression of the writers and, by extension, of their organizations.

The e-mail you write says a lot about you. It tells readers that you are thorough, accurate, and attentive—or not. It indicates that your message is to be taken seriously—or not. It implies that you know what you're talking about—or not.

In this chapter, you'll find guidelines for writing e-mail messages that convey a positive, professional image, including how to:

- Use active, concise, specific language and plain English that communicate clearly and accurately

- Write grammatically correct sentences that convey complete thoughts and flow smoothly

- Use gender-neutral language when possible

- Avoid common errors of punctuation

FOR A SEAMLESS STYLE: USE LANGUAGE THAT COMMUNICATES CLEARLY, ACCURATELY, AND CONCISELY

Sometimes you come across corporate gibberish so tortured, so triumphantly incomprehensible, you can only shake your head in admiration....

– DAVID LAZARUS, "GOBBLEDYGOOK BOILS DOWN TO LOSS OF GRACE"
San Francisco Chronicle, APRIL 3, 2005

Use Active Language

Active language is energetic and clear, while passive language weakens your writing and can confuse readers.

Here's the difference: In a passive sentence, the subject is acted upon, while in an active sentence, the subject does the acting. Notice that in the passive sentence below, the subject, or actor (the "executive committee"), comes after the verb, or action ("was made").

> *Passive*   The decision was made by the executive committee.

In an active sentence, the actor comes first, before the action:

> *Active*   The executive committee made the decision.

Here's another example. In this case, the "actor" in the active sentence is the implied "you":

> *Passive*   It would be appreciated if a summary of your speech could be received by Thursday.

> *Active*   [You] Please send us a summary of your speech by Thursday.

You can see that active sentences get the message across quickly and clearly, while passive sentences are longer and flatter in tone. In fact, one of the worst things about passive writing is that it implies the message isn't important, as in this example:

> *Passive*   A fire is being experienced in my building. It would be appreciated if this could be put out as soon as possible.

Clearly, that message would be more effective in active language:

> *Active*   My building is on fire—put it out right away!

Active language is particularly important when you are giving instructions. Which of these instructions could you follow more easily?

> *Passive*   The battery should be charged for a minimum of four hours before the equipment is put into operation. The charging of the battery can be initiated by the insertion of the dock connector into the cable that is then connected to the power source.

> *Active*   Charge the battery for at least four hours before using the equipment. Insert the dock connector into the cable and then connect the cable to the power source.

Obviously, the instructions written in active language would be easier to follow.

Some passive sentences omit the actor altogether. In fact, that omission is often deliberate.

> *Passive*   Last quarter's budget figures were overstated.

Leaving out the actor in sentences like that one raises the question of who took, is taking, or will take the action.

It's not wrong to use passive language occasionally. Sometimes you want to focus on the action, and the actor isn't very important:

> *Passive*   After a three-hour search, the missing laptop was found on a shelf in the storage cabinet.

You might occasionally use passive language to vary the rhythms of your sentences. Keep in mind, however, that too much passive language saps energy from your writing and makes it wordy. Passive language can also confuse readers.

Pointers for Using Active Language

To make sure that you use active language when you write, do the following:

PUT THE ACTOR BEFORE THE ACTION.

> *Passive*   The proposal was prepared by Martine.

> *Active*   Martine prepared the proposal.
>   (actor → action)

SAY WHO ACTED, NOT JUST WHAT WAS DONE.

> *Passive*   A new procedure has been designed for processing invoices.

> *Active*   Accounting has designed a new procedure for processing invoices.

WHEN GIVING INSTRUCTIONS, TALK DIRECTLY TO READERS. In this example, the actor is the implied "you."

> *Passive*   Your comments on the draft report are to be sent to Alex, not to me.

> *Active*   [You] Please send your comments on the draft report to Alex, not to me.

THINK ABOUT . . .

Which of the sentences below are active? Can you revise the passive sentences so they are active? If necessary, use your imagination to supply an actor. You'll find the answers at the end of this chapter.

1. In response to feedback from our patients, e-mail consultations will soon be offered for a small fee.

2. Click the link below for a Web site where you can find marker pens that don't bleed, are not toxic, and come in great colors.

3. On the attached spreadsheet, the numbers in blue are variables that can be changed by you.

4. Please submit your expense reports at least three days before the end of each month.

5. Five of my associates exceeded their sales quotas last quarter.

6. If your Basic Plan coverage is terminated by the Company for any reason, a request for Administrative Review can be made within 90 days.

7. Genes control nearly every aspect of our physiologic functions.

8. E-mail newsletters will be sent by the human resources office at least four times a year.

Use Plain English

Most of us read our e-mail very quickly. If a message is hard to understand, we're likely to skip it and go on to something that's easier to read. Even when we do take the time to read a message that's written in inflated language, jargon, overly technical language, or unfamiliar slang, we might miss or misunderstand important points.

Avoid Inflated Language

How easily can you read this e-mail excerpt?

> Per your request, attached hereto are documents describing the
> parameters of the proposed system modifications. Prior to implement-
> ing these modifications, we request your assistance in facilitating distri-
> bution of said documents to the appropriate personnel.

Perhaps what that writer is really trying to say is this:

> As you asked, I've attached a description of the proposed system
> changes. Before we begin making these changes, we would appreciate
> your help in distributing the description to all the project participants.

E. B. White said it clearly in *The Elements of Style*: "Do not be tempted by a twenty-dollar word when there is a ten-center handy, ready and able."[5] Language that is more complicated than it needs to be forces readers to translate the writing into ordinary words, and their translation might not be what you intended to say. When we write, we sometimes forget that ordinary words communicate clearly and directly and still convey a professional image.

THINK ABOUT . . .

Can you revise this sentence so it communicates more clearly? You'll have to guess at what the writer meant to say. There's a suggested revision at the end of the chapter.

> The injuries sustained by the passenger during the accident were
> the result of his failure to use the vehicle's restraining retentioning
> elements.

Use Jargon and Technical Language Cautiously

Webster's *New Collegiate Dictionary* defines jargon as a "hybrid language" that is "used for communication between specific people"—or "the technical terminology or . . . idiom of a special activity or group." [6]

The following sentence is an example of the way in which jargon fails to communicate clearly to people outside a specific group. Can you understand it?

> Since we replaced the BRK used for Wildhorse, we have not had a single re-occurrence of report timeouts with Seabrook in the ALNIB environment.

Jargon can be a handy form of shorthand—assuming that your readers understand the words, phrases, and acronyms you use. But if they don't, you might as well write in Martian. They won't even be able to use a dictionary to find the meaning of the terms they don't understand.

Similarly, for readers who understand the terminology, technical language is often the most concise, accurate way of conveying certain concepts or information. But if people don't understand the technical language you use, your writing won't make much sense.

THINK ABOUT . . .

Do you often use jargon or technical language when you write? How well do you think your readers understand the language you use?

Use Abbreviations with Caution

Don't send messages littered with "This is 4 U" and words with no vowels, like "pls snd cmmts." People at work don't speak "teenage text message."

— GABRIEL KASPER, CONSULTANT
KASPER AND ASSOCIATES

Can you understand this writer's message?

> Attchd inclds nms & adds of all sbcntrctrs in this prjct & $$ of assess-
> ment, pr yr req.

You could probably decipher the message if you worked hard enough:

> Attached includes names and addresses of all subcontractors in this
> project and cost of assessment, per your request.

By abbreviating words instead of spelling them out, the writer saved a few seconds at the reader's expense. But that kind of shorthand forces readers to figure out your abbreviations, and there's a good chance they'll miss—or misunderstand—something important.

Curtail Colloquialisms

What image do you get of the person who wrote the following?

> I'll pass this on to the head honcho, but in the end gotta say that's life
> here in the Wild West. I'm guessing there won't be any more probs but
> with deadlines hanging fire I hear ya.

It's a safe bet that most people would not think of this writer as a professional. Slang and colloquial language might be fine for an e-mail to your friends, but it's not very businesslike. Also, people in other countries—and in other age groups—probably won't understand the terms. You can never be sure where your e-mail messages will end up, so it's a good idea to use standard language. You can still keep the tone friendly and casual.

THINK ABOUT . . .

Do you often use colloquial language when you write e-mail? Do you ever use that kind of language when standard English would be more appropriate?

Cut Out the Clutter: Eliminate Unnecessary Words

Words that aren't necessary to convey meaning or tone slow readers down. Too many unnecessary words also make your writing boring and shift the focus away from the important message.

Cluttered   The attachment to this e-mail message is an example of the Member Preferences Questionnaire which is used by the Member Services Department for the purpose of conducting an evaluation of the preferences of our members for services of various types. It would be appreciated if this example questionnaire could be forwarded to the customer service team in order for it to serve as a model for the customer services questionnaire that they are in the process of developing.

(By the way, did you notice that the cluttered example uses a lot of passive language?)

Concise   I've attached an example of the questionnaire that Member Services uses to evaluate our members' preferences for various services. Please send it to the Customer Service team so they can use it as a model for the form they are developing.

Pointers for Getting Rid of Clutter

For strong, focused writing, try to eliminate every word that serves no clear purpose—every word that is not needed to convey meaning or carry tone.

USE ONLY ONE WORD FOR A ONE-WORD IDEA.

Cluttered   We are in agreement with you about the contract terms.

The client made an offer to host the meeting.

Human Resources has made a decision to redesign its Web site.

Concise   We agree with you about the contract terms.

The client offered to host the meeting.

Human Resources decided to redesign its Web site.

AVOID UNNECESSARY REPETITION. Writers have a tendency to say the same thing more than once. In particular, we tend to use repetitive phrases—several words when one or two would say the same thing. For example:

past experience	regular weekly meetings
end result	equally as effective as
ten a.m. in the morning	future plans

Here are some more examples:

Cluttered   The future site of the building site is located at the north-west corner of 7th and B streets.

Until last week, our team had the best record to date.

The sales figures during the period of January 1 and June 30 of this year compare favorably with the sales figures during the period of January 1 and June 30 of the previous year.

Concise   The building site is at the northwest corner of 7th and B streets.

Until last week, our team had the best record.

This year's January 1 – June 30 sales figures compare favorably with those of the same period of last year.

THINK ABOUT . . .

Can you tighten up the sentences below and on the next page by removing unnecessary clutter? Hint: you might also need to make some of the sentences more active. You'll find suggested revisions at the end of the chapter.

1. As you may or may not know, a majority of our employees—more than 75 per cent—have expressed the opinion that their preference would be to work flexible hours.

2. The technical support team intends to perform an evaluation of each of our departments' needs within the period of the next six months.

3. Despite the fact that our CEO is very busy, our past experience has been that she takes the ideas we express seriously.

4. It is our recommendation that you proceed to conduct a thorough review of the loans that were made by your agency during the period that began on January 1, 2004, and that ended six months later, on June 30, 2004.

5. There are thousands of hours wasted because no one can use the files which are out-of-date.

Use Specific Language

Which version of this sentence conveys the most useful information?

> *Version 1*   The building was destroyed in a disaster some time ago.
>
> *Version 2*   Fire destroyed the apartment house in March 2003.

Notice how much more information Version 2 conveys: the kind of disaster, the kind of building, and what "some time ago" means.

Here's another example:

> *Version 1*   Please complete the paperwork in a timely manner.
>
> *Version 2*   Please fill out the benefits application and return it by June 7.

Vague words such as "in a timely manner" are likely to achieve vague results. The more precise and specific your language, the easier it is for readers to understand your message—and the more likely you are to get the results you need.

THINK ABOUT . . .

Using your imagination to guess what the writer meant to say and to fill in missing details, how could you reword this sentence so it's more specific? There's a suggested revision at the end of the chapter.

> The victim suffered multiple injuries to her upper limbs and facial area that resulted in a short stay in a medical facility.

STRENGTHEN THOSE SENTENCES: USE SHORT, SIMPLE, FOCUSED SENTENCES AND GOOD GRAMMAR

E-mail is a party to which English teachers have not been invited.

— FORMER UNIVERSITY PROFESSOR R. CRAIG HOGAN
IN "WHAT CORPORATE AMERICA CAN'T BUILD: A SENTENCE"
The New York Times, DECEMBER 7, 2004

Using active, concise, specific language and plain English will go a long way toward making sure that your writing communicates clearly and forcefully. Communicating clearly and conveying a professional image also require paying attention to the way you structure your sentences.

We're not going to pretend to cover all the grammar rules in this chapter. Lots of good reference books and self-teaching guides are available (we've listed several on our Web site). But in this part of the chapter you'll find descriptions of several problems that commonly result in unprofessional e-mail messages:

- Misused modifiers

- Incomplete sentences

- Awkward and overly long sentences

- Incorrect subject-verb agreement

- Incorrect and unclear use of pronouns

> **READ YOUR ORGANIZATION'S STYLE GUIDE**
>
> Does your organization have a style guide for e-mail and other types of written communication? If so, be sure you have a copy and are familiar with its contents. If not, consider working with your colleagues to develop one.

Watch Those Modifiers

A modifier is a word or group of words that refers to or changes the meaning of (modifies) another word or group of words. Confusing or awkward sentences result when modifiers "dangle" or are misplaced.

Dangling Modifier	After meeting with me over lunch to discuss the contract, <u>the project</u> was cancelled.

As written, that sentence implies that the *project* met with the writer over lunch. The modifier is "After meeting with me over lunch to discuss the contract." But it's not clear what those words are modifying—they don't relate logically to the rest of the sentence.

To repair the sentence, you'd need to say *who* met over lunch. Here's one possibility:

Revision	After meeting with me over lunch to discuss the contract, <u>the client</u> canceled the project.

Here's another example:

Misplaced Modifier	The water from the broken water pipe <u>almost</u> flooded the entire warehouse.

Because of the placement of "almost," that sentence seems to say that the warehouse narrowly escaped being flooded. But the writer actually meant to say that the water flooded most of the warehouse. Moving the word "almost" makes the meaning clear:

Revision	The water from the broken water pipe flooded <u>almost</u> the entire warehouse.

Now it's easy to see that by putting "almost" in the wrong place in the original sentence, the writer sent the wrong message.

> *Misplaced Modifier*   The customer service representatives were informed that they would be assigned to rotating shifts for the next two months <u>by their manager</u>.

Can you tell whether the manager informed the representatives or will assign them to rotating shifts—or both? The sentence reads more clearly when the modifying words, "by their manager," are in the right place:

> *Revision*   The customer service representatives were informed by their manager that they would be assigned to rotating shifts for the next two months.

But you probably noticed that the both the original sentence and the revision in that example use passive language. Passive language often yields unclear, awkward sentences. Here's an even better revision:

> *Revision*   The manager informed the customer service representatives that she would be assigning them to rotating shifts for the next two months.

THINK ABOUT . . .

Can you underline the problem modifiers in these sentences and revise the sentences so the modifiers are in the right place? Suggested revisions appear at the end of the chapter.

1. Several consultants have recommended phasing in the changes over a one-year period including one referred by a colleague whose judgment I trust.

2. After completing the field tests of the second-generation system, decisions will need to be made about what next steps we need to take.

3. Several portfolio managers cited significant declines in interest rates in their weekly newsletters.

Use Complete Sentences

A complete sentence conveys a complete thought. A fragment is just that—part of a thought.

> Ran into John Posner the other day. Interested in joining the new venture. Would like copy of business plan ASAP. What a good opportunity!

The reader could probably figure out most of this message if he or she knew the writer well. But the last line would still be unclear—what's the "good opportunity"?

For e-mail, it's not always essential to write full sentences. For example, if you're engaging in an e-mail conversation with a colleague or a small group, or answering a quick question, a few words might convey your message just fine:

> To consider at tomorrow's meeting: deadlines, deadlines, deadlines.

> Monday, March 6—OK.

> Sure—when we get budget approval.

But even if readers can easily figure out the meaning of your abbreviated sentences, keep in mind that fragmented writing can convey a sense that your message isn't very important. If it were, you'd probably have taken the time to write complete sentences that express complete thoughts. Also, keep in mind that your readers might forward an "abbreviated" message to someone who won't be able to understand it easily.

THINK ABOUT . . .

Underline the sentence fragments in this excerpt from an e-mail. Then write out the sentences so they express complete thoughts. See the end of the chapter for a revision.

> The client expects the designs by October 1. Tight deadline for us. Need to brainstorm ideas for getting work done on time. Please bring your suggestions to Friday's meeting.

Keep Sentences Short, Simple, and Focused

A sentence that's too long is like a person who keeps talking without taking a breath:

> Attached is a revised version of the on-line catalogue which includes the feedback we have received from the reviewers who responded to our requests for comments, and even though we are expecting several additional reviews to arrive this week we thought it would be helpful for you to see what we have been able to do so far and this version should be close enough to complete for you to proceed with your own part of the project. (78 words)

Long sentences are very hard to read, especially on a computer screen. See how much easier the message is to grasp when it's broken down into shorter sentences, each conveying one primary thought.

> Attached is a revised version of the on-line catalogue. (9 words) This version includes the feedback we have received from the reviewers who responded to our requests for comments. (18 words) Even though we are expecting several additional reviews to arrive this week, we thought it would be helpful for you to see what we have been able to do so far. (31 words) This version should be close enough to complete for you to proceed with your own part of the project. (19 words)

Even though the revision is easier to read, however, it still contains two very long sentences, and the average sentence length is 19 words.

Here's one more version, edited to remove unnecessary words that add to the sentence length:

> Attached is a revised version of the on-line catalogue. (9 words) This version includes the feedback we received from reviewers. (9 words) Even though we expect several more reviews this week, we thought it would be helpful for you to see what we have done so far. (25 words) This version should be complete enough for you to proceed with your part of the project. (16 words)

Now the average sentence length is 15 words, and no sentence is longer than 25 words. The revision conveys the message quickly and clearly.

There are no hard-and-fast rules for sentence length. But here are some pointers:

- Keep the *average* length of your sentences to 15–20 words, with one primary thought per sentence. Avoid linking several thoughts with "and."

- Avoid writing sentences that are longer than 28–30 words. People often have to read overly long sentences more than once to grasp their meaning.

- Lower the average sentence length when you are conveying highly technical information and/or communicating with readers whose first language is not English.

Avoid Choppy Sentences

Sometimes the problem isn't sentences that are too long, it's sentences that are too short and choppy:

> We have received your invoice. The invoice does not include your employer I.D. number. Please send a new invoice with the employer I.D. number. Then we can process your payment.

Those four sentences can easily be combined so that the message reads more smoothly:

> The invoice you sent does not include your employer I.D. number. Please send a new invoice so we can process your payment.

Notice that each of the sentences in the revised message quickly and clearly conveys one complete thought.

THINK ABOUT . . .

Revise these sentences so that they are short enough to read easily but not choppy. Compare your revisions to the ones at the end of the chapter.

1. To enroll in an HMO Managed Care Plan, you must live in the plan's approved geographic service area, contact the plan administrator to obtain an enrollment application, then return the completed application to the plan administrator, and when your application has been approved, select a primary care provider from the list of those who contract with the plan.

2. We are pleased to submit this proposal. The proposal is to assess the City's hiring procedures. The proposal is in response to your RFP.

Make Sure That Subjects and Verbs Agree

When they are used together, a subject and verb must agree in number. If the subject is singular, the verb must be singular; if the subject is plural, the verb must be plural.

It's not always easy to identify the subject to which the verb relates. Read the sentences below. Which verb completes each sentence correctly?

1. It is the variety of customization options that (make / makes) their product so popular.
2. Neither of the designers (have / has) met the deadline.
3. Our management committee (approve / approves) the budget.
4. The public (is / are) likely to be interested in the results of our investigation.
5. E-mail is one of those technological advances that often (take / takes) more of our time than it saves.

Although it would be easy to assume that the subjects of those sentences are all plural, the subject of each sentence is actually singular. Thus, the verb must also be singular.

In these revisions, the singular subject is underlined and the singular verb appears in boldface.

1. It is the <u>variety</u> of customization options that **makes** their product so popular.
2. <u>Neither</u> of the designers **has** met the deadline.
3. Our <u>management committee</u> **approves** the budget.
4. The <u>public</u> **is** likely to be interested in the results of our investigation.
5. <u>E-mail</u> is one of those technological advances that often **takes** more of our time than it saves.

THINK ABOUT . . .

Correct any incorrect verbs in these sentences. See the end of the chapter for the answers.

1. Each of the reporters are assigned to the night desk as part of job training.

2. Every person on the investigative staff submits a detailed progress report each month.

3. The audience always appreciate a brief presentation.

4. Allen Kater, one of our group's most active members, have been nominated for an award.

5. The customer who received defective products need reassurance that we will replace them or refund her money.

Use Pronouns Correctly

The English language uses many different types of pronouns to replace nouns and other pronouns. Common pronoun problems include:

- Using "me" or "myself" when "I" is correct

- Confusing readers by using pronouns that do not clearly refer to a noun or another pronoun

- Using gender-related pronouns when both genders are represented

Me, Myself or I?

Which pronoun—me or I—would you put on each blank line in these sentences?

1. Alice, Nathan, and _____ will fly to New York on Thursday.

2. While the IT manager is away, you can speak with Michael DeBrer or _____ about any problems with your system.

I OR ME?

To decide whether "I" or "me" is correct, remove the other person from the sentence and say the sentence aloud to yourself:

> You can deliver the plans to the Production Supervisor or _____ .

> You can deliver the plans to **me**.

> You can deliver the plans to the Production Supervisor or **me**.

Here are some guidelines:

- When the pronoun is the **subject** of the action, use **I**

  > Alice, Nathan, and **I** will fly to New York on Thursday.

- When the pronoun is the **object** of the action or the preposition, use **me**

  > While the IT manager is away, you can speak with Michael DeBrer or **me** about any problems with your system.

A common mistake is to use **myself** in place of **I** or **me,** as in this example:

| *Incorrect* | The engineer and **myself** will take the prototype to the client's office. |
| *Correct* | The engineer and **I** will take the prototype to the client's office. |

WHO OR THAT?
- Use who when you are referring to people
- Use that when you are referring to animals and things

  > The associate **who** handled the sale did an excellent job, and the order **that** resulted was larger than we had expected.

THAT OR WHICH?

Generally, use that, without a comma, when pointing to something specific, and which, with a comma, when adding information that is not essential:

> Please send me the manuscript **that** is ready to be typeset.

That points to a specific manuscript—the one that is ready to be typeset.

> Please send me the manuscript, **which** I will give to the editor for review.

> The manuscript, **which** is on the table, is ready to be typeset.

Which adds information—what will be done with the manuscript in the first example, and where the manuscript is in the second example.

There are really only three situations in which you might use **myself** in business writing:

- For added emphasis

  > I **myself** would have preferred to study another option before making a decision.

- To make the point that you did something on your own

  > I spoke with each of the team members **myself**.

- When referring to yourself as you would refer to another person

  > I consider **myself** an excellent candidate for that position.

THINK ABOUT . . .

Underline any incorrect uses of I, me, or myself in the following sentences. Then correct the sentences. The answers are at the end of the chapter.

1. Danielle and myself have agreed to write the project report.

2. The software vendor spent three hours training Greg, Marcie, and I last Thursday.

3. I myself would never have agreed to the terms of that contract.

4. Our most important clients asked Pete and me to attend the product launch.

5. Please join our team and myself in the conference room tomorrow at ten a.m. for a presentation about the relocation plan.

Make Sure Pronouns Have Clear References

Pronouns that do not clearly refer to a noun or another pronoun can confuse readers:

> The engine in the delivery truck was in such bad shape that the mechanics had to replace **it**.

What did the mechanics have to replace—the engine or the truck?

> Sandra Weisman told Mona Seiple that **she** would be responsible for leading the new team.

Who would be responsible for leading the team—Sandra or Mona?

> We have approval to hire three temporary workers, and new computers will be installed this week. **This** means that we are more likely to meet our deadline.

Why are we more likely to meet the deadline—because of the temporary workers or the new computers, or both?

In those sentences, readers have no way of knowing which interpretation is correct. Not only do unclear pronoun references like those lead to confusion, they sometimes result in serious mistakes. See how much clearer the meaning is when the sentences are rewritten:

> The mechanics replaced the delivery truck's engine because it was in such bad shape.

> Sandra Weisman told Mona Seiple that Mona would be responsible for leading the new team.

> We have approval to hire three temporary workers, and new computers will be installed this week. The extra staff and computers mean that we are more likely to meet our deadline.

THINK ABOUT . . .

Underline any pronouns in these sentences that do not clearly refer to specific nouns. Then revise the sentences so that the pronoun references are clear. You might have to guess at what the writer meant to say. Corrections appear at the end of the chapter.

1. A list of energy-saving methods was enclosed with the most recent utility bill. For example, they suggested insulating the water pipes.

2. The proposal was already more than a week late when the editor found a serious error on page 16, so it had to be redone.

Use Gender-Neutral Language

Pick up almost any business communication written before 1969 and you'll find that the writer assumed that "he" was writing to an audience of men. Here's an example:

```
The ideal applicant will have a degree in business
from an accredited four-year college. In addition,
he will have worked in our industry or a related
field for at least three years. He should be able to
demonstrate an ability to solve problems and think
critically.
```

Today, it is no longer acceptable to use pronouns that imply you are speaking only about men when women are also represented. The 21st Century version of that paragraph would read:

> Ideally, applicants will have a degree in business from an accredited four-year college. In addition, they will have worked in our industry or a related field for at least three years. They should be able to demonstrate an ability to solve problems and think critically.

To keep your writing as gender-neutral as possible, use one of these techniques:

USE PLURAL INSTEAD OF SINGULAR PRONOUNS. In English, plural pronouns such as "they" and "their" do not refer to gender. Notice that we used plural pronouns to revise the sentence in the example above.

ELIMINATE THE PRONOUN ALTOGETHER. Instead of, "The manager needs to send his recommendations for budget cuts to the team in February," write, "The manager needs to recommend budget cuts to the team in February."

SPEAK DIRECTLY TO YOUR READER. Instead of, "Any client who purchases a package before the official release date will receive a discount on his invoice," write, "If you purchase a package before the official release date, you will receive a discount on your invoice."

STRUCTURE THE SENTENCE SO YOU CAN USE "WHO." Instead of, "If a new employee begins work during the last week of a month, he will attend the orientation session during the first week of the next month," write, "A new employee who begins work during the last week of a month will attend the orientation session during the first week of the next month."

> **AVOID HE/SHE AND S/HE**
>
> Attempts to keep sentences gender-neutral sometimes result in very awkward constructions. We recommend using "he and she" or "he or she" instead, and only when you can't come up with a better alternative.

EVOLVING GRAMMAR

Although still not technically correct, it's becoming increasingly acceptable to use the plural pronouns "their," "they," and "them" with singular indefinite pronouns such as "everyone." For example, instead of writing "Human Resources asked everyone to select his/her new benefits plan before March 1," most people think it would be okay to write, "Human Resources asked everyone to select their new benefits plan before March 1." Even better, you could say, "Human Resources asked all employees to select their new benefits plan before March 1."

THINK ABOUT...

Revise this sentence so the language is gender-neutral. Then check the revision at the end of the chapter.

> When referring to a policies and procedures manual, a supervisor should always make sure that his version is the latest one.

PUNCTUATE PROPERLY: USE COMMAS, SEMICOLONS, AND OTHER PUNCTUATION MARKS TO HELP CONVEY YOUR MESSAGE

Some people think that punctuation isn't important anymore. But they're wrong—punctuation always matters. Punctuation does for writing what the pauses, shifts in tone, emphasized words, and gestures do in a conversation—it helps make your meaning clear. Missing or incorrect punctuation can confuse readers; it can even change the meaning.

Notice how one little comma in the next example prevents an unpleasant implication and makes the meaning of the sentence clear:

Unclear	As you know nothing changed as a result of the investigation.
Clear	As you know, nothing changed as a result of the investigation.

The most common—and the most commonly misused—punctuation mark is the comma. Other important marks to think about are the semicolon, the colon, and the apostrophe.

!!!!!

E-mail writers seem to love exclamation marks! They're okay, but use them sparingly! They can make your writing seem very unprofessional!!!

Pointers for Using Commas[*]

AVOID COMMA SPLICES. You can (and usually should) use a comma when you join two independent clauses (complete sentences) with a coordinating conjunction (and, but, for, nor, or, so, yet). But you can't use a comma by itself to splice the sentences together:

Wrong   We can expect some changes in the project timeline, we will do our best to meet your deadline.

Right   We can expect some changes in the project timeline, but we will do our best to meet your deadline.

DON'T SET OFF ESSENTIAL INFORMATION WITH COMMAS. You can (and usually should) use commas to set off information that could be removed without changing the meaning. But don't put commas around information that needs to be there:

No Commas Wanted   All clients who have not responded to the survey should be sent a follow-up e-mail.

Taking out the words "who have not responded to the survey" would change the meaning to say that *all* clients should be sent a follow-up e-mail, not just those who have not responded. So you would not separate those words from the rest of the sentence with commas:

Commas Needed   Linda Gomez, who has been our CFO for the past five years, is leaving the company to start a business of her own.

The words "who has been our CFO for the past five years" convey extra information that could be removed without changing the meaning of the sentence. That's why you would set them off with commas.

---

[*]Commas are so tricky that we've written an entire book on the subject. *Just Commas: Nine Basic Rules* is available on our Web site (www.writeitwell.com), where you'll also find comma tips available for free download.

"DO I NEED TO USE A COMMA AFTER THE LAST ITEM IN A SERIES?"

The answer to this common question is, "Sometimes." Commas make it clear that each item in the series is a separate item. It's never wrong to use a comma before the "and" in a series, so we think that it's easier to use it all the time.

> The budget includes funds for hiring new staff, providing computer software training for everyone on the development team, and expanding the library.

DON'T USE A COMMA TO SEPARATE A GROUP OF WORDS FROM THE SUBJECT OF THE SENTENCE. Be careful not to use a comma to separate a complete sentence from a dependent clause (a group of words that depends on the rest of the sentence for its meaning):

> *Wrong*   The team leader is responsible for setting the agenda, and for scheduling the meeting.

The comma in that sentence creates a sentence fragment because the words "scheduling the meeting" don't stand on their own as a complete sentence:

> *Right*   The team leader is responsible for setting the agenda and for scheduling the meeting.

AS A RULE, USE A COMMA AFTER AN INTRODUCTORY CLAUSE. If the clause is short and there is absolutely no chance of misunderstanding, you could leave the comma out. But it's never wrong to use it:

> *Comma needed*   Geographically closer to Atlanta than Miami, Tallahassee is more like a traditional southern city than its neighbors to the south.
>
> *Comma suggested*   After a three-hour meeting(,) the directors adjourned without making a decision.

Pointers for Using Semicolons

Now, you should be warned that few adults do understand semicolons; other adults just think they understand.

— "BETWEEN A COMMA AND A PERIOD"
the new york times, NOVEMBER 7, 1999

The easiest way to think about semicolons are that they are more than commas but less than periods. They have two primary uses:

- To join two closely related independent clauses (sentences) without using a coordinating conjunction

  > Tests of the reconfigured system will begin in two weeks; we hope for better results this time.

  > We sent invitations to 500 of our most valued customers; however, only 173 people had responded by last Friday.

- To separate elements in a series that already contains commas

  > The transition will be led by Amelia Margolis, manager of marketing; Dion Trang, manager of IT; and Milas Lupchek, director of customer relations.

COLONS (:) ARE NOT THE SAME AS SEMICOLONS (;)

Colons are most commonly used to introduce something.

> Please bring the following to the meeting:
>
> – Your copy of the report
> – A bag lunch
> – Ideas for a fundraising campaign

> I have one important question: What's the location of the seminar?

You can also use a colon after the salutation on your e-mail, although these days a comma is also acceptable, and some people think it's more friendly to use a comma.

> Dear Ms. Durphy:
>
> Dear Ms. Durphy,

Pointers for Using Apostrophes

Another punctuation mark that writers often misuse is the apostrophe. Apostrophes are used to signify ownership and to replace the missing letter in contractions.

APOSTROPHES USED TO SIGNIFY OWNERSHIP. Notice that the apostrophe is placed differently, depending on whether the word that owns or possesses something is singular or plural. Generally, the apostrophe goes before the "s" when the word is singular and after the "s" when the word is plural:

> Our company's products
>
> The client's concerns
>
> Several employees' questions
>
> The computers' defects

But *be careful*: Some words are already plural in form. In those cases, the apostrophe goes *before* the "s":

> The children's books
>
> The women's careers

Also, these *possessive pronouns* do not need apostrophes because they already indicate ownership:

its	theirs	hers	his
whose	yours	ours	

USING APOSTROPHES WITH PLURAL NOUNS ENDING IN "S"

To show possession with a plural noun that ends in "s," add only an apostrophe:

> The computers' keyboards
> The Williams' shipment

APOSTROPHES THAT REPLACE THE MISSING LETTER IN CONTRACTIONS. Here are some common contractions:

It is = it's	does not = doesn't	we would = we'd
cannot = can't	do not = don't	who is = who's
I have = I've	should not = shouldn't	I will = I'll

You can use contractions to convey a casual, friendly tone:

Formal   It is a good idea to send hard copies of documents to anyone who cannot print them out before the meeting.

Casual   It's a good idea to send hard copies of documents to anyone who can't print them out before the meeting.

"ITS" AND "IT'S" ARE DIFFERENT WORDS

Be careful not to confuse the possessive pronoun "its," which needs no apostrophe, with the contraction "it's," which does.

Wrong   The taxi lost **it's** wheel coming around the curve.
Right   The taxi lost **its** wheel coming around the curve.

If you're not sure whether to use "its" or "it's," remember that an apostrophe in a contraction means something has been left out. The letter that has been left out of "it's" is the "i" in "it is." You wouldn't say, "The taxi lost it is wheel. . . ." So "its" must be the right form.

Pointers for Using Dashes and Parentheses

Dashes and parentheses make your writing more expressive. Both types of punctuation are used to set off information that is not essential to the meaning of a sentence. Dashes tend to highlight the information, while parentheses tend to minimize it or play it down. You can see how that works in the two versions of the same sentence that follow:

We are pleased to welcome Dewey Freire—former CEO of Elements.com—to our advisory board.

We are pleased to welcome Dewey Freire (former CEO of Elements.com) to our advisory board.

Tips for Using Dashes

If the information you are setting off comes in the middle of a sentence, use a dash before *and after* the phrase or clause:

> *Wrong*   The ideal candidate will have good people skills—friendliness, patience, and an ability to listen, and the ability to learn new skills quickly.

> *Right*   The ideal candidate will have good people skills—friendliness, patience, and an ability to listen—and the ability to learn new skills quickly.

> **USE HYPHENS TO CREATE A DASH**
>
> **If you can't easily create dashes on your e-mail system, it's okay to use two hyphens:**
>
> Thanks for giving me your travel dates--I'll put them on my calendar.

If the information you are setting off comes at the end of a sentence, you need to use only one dash:

> The system was out of service for six full days this month—we need to replace it immediately.

Tips for Using Parentheses

Common errors include leaving out the closing mark, enclosing too much text in parentheses, and using parentheses too often.

Be sure to use both an opening *and* a closing parenthesis:

> *Wrong*   As I mentioned, I'll be out of town (without access to e-mail or voice mail from Nov. 12 to Nov. 23.

> *Right*   As I mentioned, I'll be out of town (without access to e-mail or voice mail) from Nov. 12 to Nov. 23.

Don't overuse parentheses. The words in parentheses are usually extra information that you could either leave out, add to the main sentence, or put into a separate sentence. Notice how the parenthetical phrases interrupt this paragraph:

> Are you and Ari now viewing the Planning Guide (the one you drafted last spring) as one of the components (in addition to the Development Guide)? If I recall correctly from our last meeting (the one in the new offices on Spring Street), Ari mentioned the possibility of a separate component (the Planning Guide?).

Keep parenthetical statements short. They should never be longer than the sentence in which they are enclosed.

Use parentheses the first time you mention an acronym:

> Please send the course outline to me, care of the Education Development Department (EDD).

THINK ABOUT . . .

How many grammar and punctuation errors can you find in this paragraph? The corrected paragraph is at the end of the chapter.

> As you know the University is experiencing adverse economic times, and in our efforts to meet the challenge of these adverse times opportunities for revenue growth and increasing our income are being examined, while at the same time taking a serious look at every expense item. In that regard, I regret to inform you that one of the expenses that are going to be eliminated are: we will no longer be able to pay for your parking while teaching. It was felt that in the past at least some of the of inconvenience brought about by inadequate parking facilities near the University could be offset by us, we sincerely regret that we can no longer do so.
>
> (If any instructor feels that he is unduly and inappropriately burdened by the decision that has been made by us. He should contact the Office of Faculty Affairs.

APPLY WHAT YOU'VE LEARNED

1. Print out five (or more) e-mail messages that you have written recently. Choose samples that are typical of your writing and that are at least a couple of paragraphs long. (If you write only very short messages, print out ten of them.)

   Review the messages, paying attention to the following:

   • *Active language and plain English.* Circle any examples you find of passive language and twenty-dollar words (pompous language). Also circle examples of jargon or technical language that readers might not have understood. Decide what kinds of changes you should make, based on what you learned in this chapter.

   • *Clutter.* Circle any unnecessary words. Decide what changes you could make to tighten up your writing.

   • *Sentence problems, grammar, and punctuation.* Look for any problems with sentences, grammar, or punctuation and correct them.

   On the lines below, describe three problems you found that you will pay attention to whenever you write.

   _____

   _____

   _____

   _____

   _____

   _____

   _____

2. Look through several of your own and your colleagues' e-mail messages. What jargon and technical language do you use in your business or your area of the company? List the jargon and technical terms that you need to translate into plain English when you write to people outside your immediate organization.

_____

_____

_____

_____

_____

3. Do a word count of your sentences. Select ten sentences, either from one long e-mail or several shorter ones. Copy and paste the sentences into your word processing program and use the Tools function to find the average number of words in the sentences, or find the average by hand.

   • What is the average number of words in those ten sentences? _____

   • How many sentences have more than 28–30 words? _____

   • If the average is more than 20 words per sentence, look for sentences that have too many thoughts joined together with "and." Revise one of them into shorter sentences with one thought per sentence.

   • If the average is less than ten words per sentence, look for sentences that can be combined and combine two or more of them.

4. Based on what you've learned in this chapter, decide what changes you need to make to keep your writing professional and clear. Write out a contract for yourself that specifies at least five things you will do during the next six weeks and post the contract where you can see it easily. There's a sample on the next page.

CONTRACT WITH MYSELF #2

Today's Date _____

During the next six weeks, I will do the following to make sure that my writing presents a professional image of myself and my organization:

_____

_____

_____

_____

_____

_____

_____

_____

_____

_____

_____

_____

(Your Signature)

Answers to Practice Exercises

USE ACTIVE LANGUAGE (Page 102)

Sentences 2, 4, 5, and 7 are active.

1. In response to feedback from our patients, e-mail consultations will soon be offered for a small fee.

   Revision: In response to feedback from our patients, our office will soon offer e-mail consultations for a small fee.

2. Click the link below for a Web site where you can find marker pens that don't bleed, are not toxic, and come in great colors.

3. On the attached spreadsheet, the numbers in blue are variables that can be changed by you.

   Revision: On the attached spreadsheet, the numbers in blue are variables that you can change.

4. Please submit your expense reports at least three days before the end of each month.

5. Five of my associates exceeded their sales quotas last quarter.

6. If your Basic Plan coverage is terminated by the Company for any reason, a request for Administrative Review can be made within 90 days.

   Revision: If the Company terminates your Basic Plan coverage for any reason, you can request an Administrative Review within 90 days.

7. Genes control nearly every aspect of our physiologic functions.

8. E-mail newsletters will be sent by the human resources office at least four times a year.

   Revision: The human resources office will send e-mail newsletters at least four times a year.

USE PLAIN ENGLISH (Page 103)

Original. The injuries sustained by the passenger during the accident were the result of his failure to use the vehicle's restraining retentioning elements.

Possible revisions:

The passenger was injured during the accident because he didn't use the seat belt.

The passenger's injuries resulted from his failure to use a seat belt.

REDUCE CLUTTER (Page 107)

Here are some ways to tighten up these sentences:

1. As you may ~~or may not~~ know, ~~a majority of our employees~~ more than 75 per cent of our employees have ~~expressed the opinion~~ said that they would prefer ~~to work~~ flexible hours.

2. The technical support team intends to ~~perform an evaluation of each of~~ evaluate our departments' needs within the ~~period of the~~ next six months.

3. ~~Despite the fact that~~ Although our CEO is very busy, our ~~past~~ experience ~~has been that~~ indicates that she takes ~~the~~ our ideas ~~we express~~ seriously.

4. ~~It is our recommendation~~ We recommend that you ~~proceed to conduct a~~ thoroughly review ~~of~~ the loans that ~~were~~ your agency made ~~by your agency during the period that began on~~ between January 1~~, 2004,~~ and ~~that ended six months later, on~~ June 30, 2004.

5. ~~There are~~ Thousands of hours are wasted because no one can use the out-of-date files. ~~which are out of date.~~

BE SPECIFIC (Page 109)

The original sentence is so vague that it's hard to know exactly what the writer meant. The revision shows one possibility.

Original. The victim suffered multiple injuries to her upper limbs and facial area that resulted in a short stay in a medical facility.

Revision. The 35-year-old woman suffered a broken right arm, a cracked left wrist, and a broken jaw. Her injuries resulted in a three-day hospital stay.

PUT MODIFIERS IN THE RIGHT PLACE (Page 111)

The problem modifiers are underlined.

1. Several consultants have recommended phasing in the changes over a one-year period <u>including one referred by a colleague whose judgment I trust</u>.

2. <u>After completing the field tests of the second-generation system</u>, decisions will need to be made about what next steps we need to take.

3. Several portfolio managers cited significant declines in interest rates <u>in their weekly newsletters</u>.

Those sentences would be clearer and less awkward with the following revisions:

1. Several consultants, including one referred by a colleague whose judgment I trust, have recommended phasing in the changes over a one-year period.

2. After completing the field tests of the second-generation system, the designers will need to make decisions about what next steps we need to take.

3. In their weekly newsletters, several portfolio managers cited significant declines in interest rates.

WRITE COMPLETE SENTENCES (Page 112)

Below the original excerpt is one way to revise it into complete sentences.

Original. The client expects the designs by October 1. <u>Tight deadline for us. Need to brainstorm ideas for getting work done on time.</u> Please bring your suggestions to Friday's meeting.

Revision. The client expects the designs by October 1. That's a tight deadline for us, so we need to brainstorm ideas for getting the work done on time. Please bring your suggestions to Friday's meeting.

KEEP SENTENCES SHORT BUT NOT CHOPPY (Page 114)

Your revisions might be similar to the ones shown below.

1. To enroll in an HMO Managed Care Plan, you must live in the plan's approved geographic service area, contact the plan administrator to obtain an enrollment application, then return the completed application to the plan administrator, and when your application has been approved, select a primary care provider from the list of those who contract with the plan.

   Revision: To enroll in an HMO Managed Care Plan, you must live in the plan's approved geographic service area. Contact the plan administrator for an enrollment application, then return the completed application to the administrator. When your application has been approved, select a primary care provider from the list of those who contract with the plan.

2. We are pleased to submit this proposal. The proposal is to assess the City's hiring procedures. The proposal is in response to your RFP.

   Revision: In response to your RFP, we are pleased to submit this proposal to assess the City's hiring procedures.

CHECK FOR SUBJECT-VERB AGREEMENT (Page 116)

Sentence 2 is correct.

1. Each of the reporters ~~are~~ **is** assigned to the night desk as part of job training.

2. Every person on the investigative staff **submits** a detailed progress report each month.

3. The audience always ~~appreciate~~ **appreciates** a brief presentation.

4. Allen Kater, one of our group's most active members, ~~have~~ **has** been nominated for an award.

5. The customer who received defective products ~~need~~ **needs** reassurance that we will replace them or refund her money.

USE I, ME, OR MYSELF? (Page 119)

Sentences 3 and 4 are correct.

1. Danielle and ~~myself~~ **I** have agreed to write the project report.
2. The software vendor spent three hours training Greg, Marcie, and ~~I~~ **me** last Thursday.
3. I **myself** would never have agreed to the terms of that contract.
4. Our most important clients asked Pete and **me** to attend the product launch.
5. Please join our team and ~~myself~~ **me** in the conference room tomorrow at ten a.m. for a presentation about the relocation plan.

MAKE SURE PRONOUN REFERENCES ARE CLEAR (Page 120)

Here are suggested corrections:

1. A list of energy-saving methods was enclosed with the most recent utility bill. For example, <u>they</u> suggested insulating the water pipes.

   Revision: A list of energy-saving methods was enclosed with the most recent utility bill. For example, ~~they~~ **the utility company** suggested insulating the water pipes.

2. The proposal was already more than a week late when the editor found a serious error on page 16, so <u>it</u> had to be redone.

   Revision: The proposal was already more than a week late when the editor found a serious error on page 16, so ~~it~~ **the entire section** had to be redone.

KEEP YOUR LANGUAGE GENDER-NEUTRAL (Page 122)

When referring to a policies and procedures manual, ~~a supervisor~~ **supervisors** should always make sure that ~~his~~ **their** version is the latest one.

USE CORRECT GRAMMAR AND PUNCTUATION (Page 129)

There are many ways to improve this paragraph. Here's one of them:

As you know, the University is experiencing adverse economic times~~, and~~. ~~In~~ In our efforts to meet ~~the~~ this challenge, ~~of these adverse times,~~ we are examining opportunities for ~~revenue growth and~~ increasing our income. ~~are being examined, while at the same time taking a serious look~~ We are also looking seriously at every expense item. In that regard, I regret to inform you that ~~one of the expenses that are going to be eliminated are:~~ we will no longer be able to pay for your parking while you are teaching. ~~It was felt that in the past~~ We hoped to offset at least some of the inconvenience brought about by inadequate parking facilities near the University, ~~could be offset by us,~~ but we sincerely regret that we can no longer do so.

(If ~~any instructor~~ you feel~~s that he is~~ unduly ~~and inappropriately~~ burdened by ~~the~~ this decision, ~~that has been made by us. He should~~ please contact the Office of Faculty Affairs.)

NOTES

_____

_____

_____

_____

_____

_____

_____

_____

_____

_____

_____

_____

_____

_____

_____

_____

_____

NOTES

5

CAUTIONARY TALES

Last year, the inability to produce subpoenaed e-mail resulted in million dollar . . . lawsuits against U.S. companies. . . . 24% of organizations have had employee e-mail subpoenaed, and 15% of companies have gone to court to battle lawsuits triggered by employee e-mail. . . . Increasingly, employers are . . . firing workers who violate computer privileges. Fully 26% of employers have terminated employees for e-mail misuse . . . 2% have dismissed workers for inappropriate instant messenger (IM) chat [and] nearly 2% have fired workers for offensive blog content—including posts on employees' personal home-based blogs.

AMERICAN MANAGEMENT ASSOCIATION (AMA) AND THE EPOLICY INSTITUTE 2006
WORKPLACE E-MAIL, INSTANT MESSAGING & BLOG SURVEY.

Neal Patterson, the chief executive of the Cerner Corporation in Kansas City, Missouri, sent 400 managers an angry e-mail, berating them for not getting more than 40 hours of work a week out of their employees: "The parking lot is sparsely used at 8 a.m.; likewise at 5 p.m . . . you have a problem and you will fix it or I will replace you. . . ." After the . . . e-mail [was] posted on a Yahoo message board, Cerner stock declined 22 percent.

FROM "STINGING OFFICE MEMO BOOMERANGS"
EDWARD WONG, *THE NEW YORK TIMES*, APRIL 5, 2001

E-mail is risky business indeed. Angry messages sent in the heat of the moment can damage relationships with colleagues and clients. Rude, abrupt messages lead to misunderstandings that can have serious consequences. Every week we hear about how the wrong e-mail sent to the wrong person (or people) has gotten an individual or an organization in trouble.

It's a fact that misuse of e-mail can harm you professionally and cost your organization in terms of money and reputation. That's what this chapter is about: the bad things that can happen when we neglect to consider e-mail's potential for causing damage.

QUICK QUIZ

Let's see how much you already know. Which of these statements are true?

1. It's safe to convey confidential information to a trusted colleague in an e-mail as long as you check the address carefully before sending it.

2. Your employer has a right to monitor your e-mail.

3. Like written documents, e-mail can be subpoenaed as evidence in a lawsuit.

4. Deleting an e-mail message is like shredding a document—you can feel confident that no one will be able to see it.

5. You can get fired for using your company's e-mail to send obscene material.

Read on to see which statements are true. (If you're feeling impatient, you can flip to page 152 for the answers.)

E-MAIL IS A PUBLIC MEDIUM

I was furious with my boss. She'd taken an idea of mine and presented it as her own. Without thinking, I wrote a message to three of my colleagues, complaining about the bum rap I'd gotten. I guess I wanted someone to know that the idea was mine, not hers. The next day my boss confronted me with a copy of the e-mail, which one of my colleagues had forwarded to her manager. Talk about an awkward situation. . . .

— GABE MADWAY, FACULTY SERVICES
USF SCHOOL OF LAW

Conveying a message via e-mail just isn't the same as sealing it into an envelope or delivering to someone on a secure phone line. E-mail is a *public* medium. Think of it as sending a post-card, shouting down the hall, or talking on a cell phone that is being monitored in a van parked outside the building.

Many people are lulled into a false sense of security by putting disclaimers on their e-mail, such as, "This e-mail is strictly confidential. . . ." Others think that they can protect confidentiality by putting "DO NOT FORWARD" in bold letters at the top of a message.

But no matter how carefully you address a message, how many cautions and disclaimers you include, or how many security precautions you take, there's always a risk that people other than your intended recipient(s) will see your e-mail. Your recipients might deliberately or accidentally send the message to someone else, or they might deliberately or accidentally include your original message when they send a copy of their reply to someone. The people who monitor your organization's system can easily see your e-mail. In fact, anyone with rudimentary technical knowledge would have little difficulty getting copies of the e-mail you send and receive.

E-MAIL IS PERMANENT

Internal Energy Department e-mail messages written in preparation for seeking a license to open a nuclear waste repository at Yucca Mountain in Nevada show that the department made false claims about how it carried out its work. . . . The Energy Department has not released the messages. . . . But . . . a lawyer for the State of Nevada, which opposes the project, provided The New York Times *with copies. . . .*

— MATTHEW L. WALD
"E-MAIL SHOWS FALSE CLAIMS ABOUT TESTS AT NEVADA NUCLEAR SITE"
THE NEW YORK TIMES, MARCH 20, 2005

You can destroy a document by feeding it into a shredder. It's not so easy with e-mail. Simply sending a message to the trash doesn't make it disappear. For one thing, the message lingers in your trash folder until you empty it—which many of us forget to do. And emptying the trash doesn't necessarily delete all traces of the message. You might have inadvertently kept a backup copy. Your organization is likely to have a backup copy. Enough of the message might still be on your hard drive so that someone could resurrect it. And of course, the recipient has a copy, as does anyone to whom the recipient might have forwarded the message. Suffice it to say, once you've written and sent an e-mail, you must think of it as forming part of a potentially public, permanent record.

THINK ABOUT . . .

Have you ever been surprised to find that a message you thought you had deleted turned up again? Do you routinely keep copies of messages that other people forward to you? Do you think that anyone might be surprised to find that you had copies of messages they'd sent to someone else?

YOUR ORGANIZATION OWNS YOUR E-MAIL

Nearly 84 percent of the employees surveyed indicated that they regularly send non-work-related e-mails each day … Employees often mistakenly believe that their use of the Internet and e-mail at the workplace is private when, in fact, courts have found no reasonable expectation of privacy in such use and have consistently permitted employers to monitor and review employee activity.

– CHARLES J. MUHL

MONTHLY LABOR REVIEW, FEBRUARY 2003

You'd think that because you're the author of an e-mail message, it belongs to you. But federal law allows organizations to monitor the e-mail sent or received using their systems to make sure that it complies with the law and regulatory requirements and meets certain standards.

Under most circumstances, this monitoring can include the personal e-mail you send or receive at work. The Federal Electronic Communications Privacy Act, enacted in 1986 to amend federal wiretapping laws and give some protection to electronic communications, doesn't do much to protect your right to use a company-provided system for personal e-mail. Increasingly, company e-mail policies stipulate that the company has the right to monitor *all* the e-mail its employees send.

You might have agreed to adhere to your company's e-mail policy when you began work. If you're like most people, however, you never really read what that policy had to say. Do it now. Make sure you understand the extent to which your employer has the right to monitor the e-mail you send. Even if your company has no e-mail policy, we suggest that you think twice before putting anything into an e-mail that you wouldn't want your boss to see.

HOW SECURE IS SECURE?

It's possible to scramble an e-mail message—to encrypt it so that only a recipient with the right "code" can read it. Encrypting a message reduces the chance that someone who receives it by accident can read it.

But it's best not to get lulled into a false sense of security. Codes are made to be broken. If what you're writing is sensitive, private, or confidential, and if there is any chance that your message could end up in a court of law, it pays to think carefully before putting that information into an e-mail. The more serious the consequences of a security breach, the more carefully you'll want to consider finding another way to communicate the message. It helps to ask yourself, "What might happen if this message got into the hands of [*fill in the blank*]?"

E-MAIL LANDMINES

My friend (I'll call him Byron) worked for a nonprofit organization and his wife (Sara) worked for a community foundation. The nonprofit was going after a big grant. Sara sent Byron some confidential information about the proposal process that gave his group a real advantage. When Sara's boss accidentally saw the e-mail, Byron's group's proposal was eliminated from consideration. They both kept their jobs, but they had done real damage to their reputations.

— DEBRA NELSON, CAMPAIGN MANAGER
AMERICAN CONSERVATORY THEATER

The Chevron Corporation agreed to pay $2.2 million to settle a class action lawsuit by women who claimed that sexually offensive jokes, comments, and e-mail messages created a threatening work environment. The offensive e-mail messages included one that was titled, "25 reasons why beer is better than women."

— FROM TAMAR LEWIN, "DEBATE CENTERS ON DEFINITION OF HARASSMENT"
the New York Times, MARCH 22, 1998, AND WWW.ATWEBO.COM/TECHNOLOGY

[Former District Attorney Dinallo] viewed e-mails as potentially an even better form of evidence [than wiretaps]. "E-mails are more direct," he explained. "They are casual, but intimate. . . . It is like a water-cooler conversation caught on the record."

— JOHN CASSIDY, "THE INVESTIGATION"
THE NEW YORKER, APRIL 7, 2003

Partly because e-mail is so public and so permanent, its misuse can cause real damage. Interpersonal relationships are damaged; confidences are betrayed; company secrets are revealed; employees lose their reputations and even their jobs; and organizations become embroiled in costly lawsuits.

The culprits include:

ANGRY, RUDE, ABRUPT E-MAIL THAT AFFECTS WORKING RELATIONSHIPS. As we said earlier, people often say things in e-mail that they would not have said in person, at least not in the same way. They vent their anger and pour out their feelings, then click on "send" without stopping to reread the message.

How would you feel if you received this e-mail?

> You said you'd get me the sales figures last Wednesday and THEY'RE NOT HERE YET. You never get me anything I ask for on time. How am I supposed to meet my deadlines if you're always late with the information???? You've got to get them to me TODAY!!!

Always keep in mind the advice we gave you earlier: if you're feeling angry or upset, use your word processor to draft the message and read it carefully before sending.

OFFENSIVE E-MAIL THAT CREATES A "HOSTILE WORKPLACE." In a casual water-cooler conversation, people often say things they would not say in public. They sometimes make remarks that are—or could be interpreted to be—sexually explicit or racist, and they sometimes make comments that refer to other people's gender, age, sexual orientation, religion or political beliefs, national origin, or disability.

> **TROUBLE FROM ATTACHMENTS**
>
> Documents you attach to an e-mail message can get you into just as much trouble as the e-mail itself. So think twice before attaching that joke sheet to the message you're forwarding to your buddy.

In other words, the sense that e-mail is more like a private conversation than a written communication sometimes leads people to say things that can be offensive to others. Among the common culprits are jokes and "funny" stories that poke fun at an individual or a group.

Out of respect for your fellow employees and to avoid getting you and your organization embroiled in a "hostile workplace" lawsuit, follow your organization's guidelines when deciding what remarks or statements you can include in an e-mail. If you're not sure what those guidelines are, or what they mean, consult your human resources representative.

BREACH OF CONFIDENTIALITY. As we've discussed, e-mail is not the appropriate way to communicate secret, proprietary, or private information. For example, putting your

LEARN THE RULES

If you work in an area of government or an industry that is subject to regulatory oversight, including health care and financial services, you need to be especially careful about what you put into e-mail messages and how you manage your e-mail. Among other things, you need to comply with regulations relating to confidentiality and privacy, as well as with those that cover deletion and storage of e-mail messages.

company's pricing strategies into an e-mail message could give competitors an advantage—and cost you your job—if the e-mail reaches the wrong people. And disclosing a client's proprietary information or an employee's medical condition could land you and your organization in court.

E-MAIL THAT UNWITTINGLY COMMITS THE ORGANIZATION TO SOMETHING. Because e-mail is written communication, an e-mail message in which you agree to perform a task could commit the organization to do so under certain circumstances.

DEFAMATORY OR LIBELOUS STATEMENTS. E-mail that contains lies or untrue statements that damage the good reputation of an individual or an organization are evidence of libel that can be used in court.

If You Receive Offensive, Confidential, or Defamatory E-Mail

You can control the content of the e-mail you send. It's harder to make sure that other people do not include you when sending inappropriate or illegal messages.

If you receive an e-mail that you believe falls into the categories we've discussed above, do the following:

- Leave the e-mail in your inbox
- Inform your human resources department or the people responsible for enforcing your organization's e-mail policy
- Depending on the circumstances, ask the sender not to send you such messages in the future

DID I REALLY SAY THAT?

One scary thing about e-mail is that people can make changes to your messages before forwarding them on to someone else. Even if those changes are made with good intentions—to condense or clarify the information, for example—they could change your meaning.

THINK ABOUT . . .

Have you ever received an e-mail that made you angry or upset? One that you found offensive? One that revealed proprietary information or the details of someone's private life? How did you feel about that e-mail? Were there any consequences?

Disclaimers

Many organizations require that cautionary information, including disclaimers such as the one below, be included on every e-mail message that leaves the premises:

> This message, including any attachments, contains confidential information intended for a specific individual and purpose, and is protected by law. If you are not the intended recipient, please contact the sender immediately by reply e-mail and destroy all copies. You are hereby notified that any disclosure, copying, or distribution of this message, or the taking of any action based on it, is strictly prohibited.

Certainly these notices can be useful, and they might offer some legal protection. But not only do disclaimers add a lot of verbiage to your messages, they are no guarantee that the content of an e-mail won't get you and your organization into trouble.

A disclaimer might help your case if something you write lands you or the organization in court, and there's always a chance that someone who is thinking of filing a lawsuit will be deterred by the presence of a disclaimer. No disclaimer, however, will protect you or your organization against a libelous statement.

Because even the most carefully written disclaimers offer only the possibility of protection, it's best not to rely on them. Instead, avoid using e-mail to communicate information that should not be made public.

SETTING UP AN E-MAIL POLICY

Every organization needs an e-mail policy that lays out the standards and clarifies the "do's" and "don'ts." A reasonable, clearly written policy that is provided to and acknowledged by everyone who uses the organization's e-mail system or sends e-mail on the organization's behalf goes a long way toward preventing problems that are not only embarrassing but can lead to lawsuits.

Your e-mail policies need to be carefully thought through and carefully written. In this section, we've offered some points to consider. For more detail, including legal implications and sample policies, consult one of the organizations that specialize in developing e-policies. We've listed some resources and provided some links on our Web site.

> **DEVELOP E-MAIL GUIDELINES FOR YOUR GROUP**
>
> If your organization has no e-mail policy, you can work with your colleagues or project team to develop guidelines for your group. For example, you might specify which messages should be distributed to everyone, which issues should not be dealt with by e-mail, and what "reasonable response time" means. You could also establish writing standards for the e-mail sent to people outside the group or organization.

What an E-Mail Policy Should Cover

Among other things, an e-mail policy should clearly explain what constitutes "permissible" use of the organization's e-mail system. It needs to describe in detail what is meant by "inappropriate" and "illegal" e-mail. It should inform employees that their e-mail messages are not confidential or private and tell them whether and how the organization will monitor the e-mail they send.

Depending on your organization's specific needs, a policy should answer these kinds of questions:

- Can I use the organization's e-mail system to send and receive personal messages?
- What kinds of messages should I keep? For how long?

- Will the organization monitor all the e-mail I send and receive? If not, what e-mail is subject to monitoring? When and how?

- Under what circumstances can I forward a message I receive?

- What content is not acceptable? What content is prohibited?

- Do I need to append disclaimers or warnings to any of my e-mail messages? What disclaimers or warnings? Under what circumstances?

- How should I sign my messages?

- What should I do if I receive inappropriate messages?

- What are the consequences if I ignore the e-mail policy?

- Who should I contact with questions about e-mail use?

In addition, a policy should address all or some of the following:

- Security issues, including the proper use of e-mail accounts and passwords

- Writing standards

- E-mail etiquette ("netiquette")

- Housekeeping, including automatic deletion of stored messages

- Protection from spam and viruses

- The use of attachments

Enforcing Your E-mail Policy

No matter how comprehensive and clearly written, an e-mail policy is useful only if it can be enforced. Simply sending out the policy with a memo to employees isn't enough. You need to

---

COMPANY NOT OBLIGED TO MONITOR MAIL

Your e-mail policy should state clearly that the company has the right to monitor employees' e-mail. But it should also state that the company is not *obliged* to monitor e-mail. Without that clause, it might be possible to argue that the organization has taken on the responsibility of protecting employees from every harmful or inappropriate e-mail that slips through the system.

know that people have read it and understand all its provisions. Otherwise, you'll find it difficult or impossible to enforce.

Here are some ways to make sure that everyone knows about and understands your policy:

- Go over the e-mail policy with *every* person who uses your e-mail system or communicates with others on your organization's behalf. Provide training. Set up small-group discussions to review the policy. Make managers, supervisors, and team leaders responsible for ensuring that every member of their staff or team is familiar with the policy.

- Obtain a dated signature from each person acknowledging that he or she has read and understood the policy.

- Include the e-mail policy in new-hire orientation materials, human resources policy manuals, and other documents.

- When setting up a new user on the system, make sure that the person has read and understands the policy before you issue a user I.D. and password.

- Provide regular reminders—for example, periodically send out messages highlighting one or another aspect of the e-mail policy; include an automatic reminder message that comes up every time a user logs on to the system.

Keep Your Policy Current

An e-mail policy should be an evolving document. Review it regularly to see what changes are needed to keep it up-to-date. For example, changes might be needed in response to new technology or new regulations, or you might need to expand or clarify certain parts of the policy. It's helpful to put one person in charge of reviewing and revising the e-mail policy.

By the way, when you make changes, be sure to tell people about them and make sure they understand them.

APPLY WHAT YOU LEARN

1. Randomly select 20 messages that you have saved in e-mail folders. Would the tone and content of any of those messages be likely to upset or anger the recipient? Could anything in the message be offensive to another person? Do any of the messages include confidential or private information?

   Use the lines below to list three steps you'll take to make sure that your e-mail follows the guidelines in this chapter:

   _____

   _____

   _____

   _____

   _____

   _____

2. Does your company have an e-mail policy? Get a copy of that policy and read it carefully. Highlight the points that are most important to you. If possible, discuss the policy with your team, group, or manager.

3. Work with your colleagues to develop e-mail guidelines and standards for the messages you send to one another and for those that you send to people outside your team, group, or organization.

   ANSWERS TO QUICK QUIZ on page 142: Statements #2, 3, and 5 are true.

NOTES

NOTES

THE BACK OF THE BOOK

LEARNING MORE ABOUT COMMUNICATING IN WRITING

Learning to write clearly doesn't stop with one book, or one workshop, or one class. Learning to write is a lifelong pursuit, and you can always get better.

Here are some ways in which you can continue to improve your writing skills:

USE WHAT YOU'VE LEARNED. People often spend time and money on books and courses and then ignore everything they've learned. Consciously and consistently use what you've learned in this book. You'll find that all your written communications will continue to improve, so that they achieve the results you want and present a professional image of you and your organization.

KEEP LEARNING. Every writing book you read and every writing class you take will help you refine your skills. Keep on reading about writing. Take some business writing workshops or classes—if your organization doesn't offer writing skills training, you'll find useful courses at your local community college or university extension. There are also some excellent self-study courses, both on line and in workbook format.

ASSESS YOUR WRITING. Schedule time every few weeks to reread some of your recent e-mail messages and other documents you've written, using the checklists on our Web site as a guide for assessing your writing.

It can also be helpful to read your writing aloud to get a sense of the tone and see whether the sentences and paragraphs flow smoothly Look at what you've written from the reader's point of view to make sure that you've used the right tone, gotten the main point across clearly, answered all the reader's questions, organized the information logically, and presented the information so it is easy to read.

BE OBSERVANT. You can learn a lot from paying attention to other people's writing. When you read something that seems very easy to understand or very difficult to follow, ask yourself what the writer did that made the writing work or what the writer should have done differently.

GET FEEDBACK. Other people often see things that we miss. Find a colleague whose judgment you trust, and periodically ask that person to give you specific feedback on your writing.

LEARNING MORE ABOUT USING E-MAIL SOFTWARE

Many of us who use e-mail every day still find that its inner workings remain somewhat mysterious. More importantly, we don't always work as productively as we could because we aren't aware of all the features our e-mail software provides or we don't know how to use them.

Here are some suggestions:

TAKE A TOUR OF YOUR SOFTWARE. If you haven't done so already, look through all your menus to see what's there. Pay special attention to the Help and Tools menus.

READ YOUR ON-SCREEN USER GUIDE. If your software includes a user guide, it can help you learn what features are available and how to use them. The guide's table of contents can direct you to specific features.

CONSULT THE CONSULTANTS. If you work for a large organization, get to know the people who provide technical support. Even if no one has formal responsibility for answering questions related to e-mail, some of your colleagues will know much more than others. If you work in a small office or on your own, professional computer consultants and friends who are technically knowledgeable are great resources.

GOOGLE IT. There's a tremendous amount of information available on the Web. If your Help menu or user guide doesn't answer your questions, use a search engine such as Google or Yahoo! Search. Make your search as specific as possible. Instead of "attachments," enter something like, "how to compress Word files when attaching them to an e-mail."

EDUCATE YOURSELF. Does your organization offer workshops, classes, or tutorials to help staff members use e-mail productively? If so, take them. If not, look for learning opportunities in your community. There are also lots of learning resources on line.

A FEW TECH FAQs

As we mentioned in the Introduction, there's far too much to say about the technical aspect of e-mail for us to do more than touch on a few salient points. We've addressed some common questions below. You'll find more information—and some links—on our Web site.

About Message Formats

Most e-mail programs, such as Microsoft Outlook, are able to send and receive messages in three different formats: HTML, RTF, and plain text. Here are brief descriptions:

HTML (HYPERTEXT MARK-UP LANGUAGE). This is the computer language that is used to create Web pages. With HTML, you can use different fonts, bullets, numbering, alignment, horizontal lines, and graphics to produce your e-mail message. Most popular e-mail programs support HTML.

RTF (RICH TEXT FORMAT). RTF is a standard format that supports some text formatting, including bullets and alignment.

PLAIN TEXT. This format allows you to use only the standard keyboard letters, numbers, and symbols. It contains no embedded format or layout information.

What's important to remember is that when you use HTML and RTF, some recipients may not be able to see your elegant formatting. For example, if your recipient's e-mail program doesn't understand HTML, it automatically displays the message as plain text. Also, HTML-formatted messages can allow viruses to sneak into your computer, so some people choose to block the display of messages in that format.

Unless you are certain that a reader has the necessary software or will open an HTML message, stick with plain text. You can create a nice, clear bulleted list by using asterisks or hyphens, as we've done with some of the examples in this book. If the formatting is important, send the information as an attachment.

Reading Your Mail On Line

Viruses can find their way into your computer by hooking themselves onto e-mail messages. One way to protect your computer is to read and manage all your mail on line instead of downloading it. You can always save or copy specific messages to a folder on your computer's hard drive.

In addition to protecting your computer from viruses, Web mail lets you read and manage your e-mail from any computer that can be hooked up to the Internet, no matter where you are in the world.

Web mail has are some disadvantages, however. You might not be able to retrieve e-mail from your corporate e-mail system, and you probably won't have access to the full array of features that e-mail software provides. Most Web mail services also have storage limits—if you exceed them, new messages might be turned away and/or your saved mail might be deleted.

About Contacts and Address Books

You can use your e-mail software to store correspondents' names, e-mail addresses, telephone numbers, fax numbers, Web addresses, mailing addresses, and other information. You might also be able to set up links with documents and other files that relate to specific individuals.

Once you've set up a correspondent's information, you can enter the person's e-mail address in a message with a click of your mouse—or simply type the person's "nickname" on the TO line. Most software will also let you set up a "favorites" list to streamline the process of addressing messages to regular correspondents.

You can also use the names in your address book to create distribution lists, or groups, for people to whom you frequently send the same message. Give each distribution list a unique name—"Production Team," "Reorganization Committee"—so you can find it easily. Some e-mail software has a setting you can use to hide all the addresses, and there are "mass mail programs" that conceal addresses. Type "mass e-mail program" into a search engine and see what you can find.

About Flagging Messages and Setting Importance Level

Most e-mail software will let you add symbols and comments to messages that give you or your recipient extra information. You can flag a message for yourself with a date for following up; add a symbol that tells recipients a message is private, personal, or confidential; and/or mark a message so your recipient knows that it is important or urgent. Look under "flagging messages" and "setting importance level" or "priority" on your Help menu. Keep in mind, however, that too many symbols cancel each other out, and too many messages marked "urgent" lower the value of the "urgent" mark.

About Security

The most important thing to remember about security is that you can never guarantee that people other than the intended readers won't read the e-mail you send. You can reduce the possibility, but you can't eliminate it altogether.

That said, there are some ways to protect your most confidential e-mail communications:

ENCRYPT MESSAGES. When you encrypt an e-mail, you scramble the content so that only people who have the right key or identification can unscramble it. Other people receive only gibberish. Look up "security" or "encryption" on the Help menu, or type "encrypt my e-mail" into a search engine.

MARK MESSAGES "PRIVATE" OR "CONFIDENTIAL." Some software programs allow you to mark a message "private." Ostensibly, that means no one else can change the message after you send it. But it doesn't necessarily mean that no one other than the recipient can see the message. Check your Help or Tools menus for more information.

About Spam

We've all become increasingly aware of the problems caused by spam, or junk mail. Spam is not only annoying, it's often the source of destructive viruses. Here are a few things to know:

USE A GOOD SPAM FILTER. Set up your software's spam filter so that most, if not all, of the junk messages that come your way are diverted to a separate folder. You can also purchase some pretty good spam-blocking software that lets you decide what level of filtering you want and identify specific kinds of messages or messages from specific addresses that you don't want to receive. Unwanted messages will be sent into a spam or junk mail folder. It's a good idea to check that folder from time to time to see whether messages you need have been incorrectly identified as junk.

NEVER OPEN A MESSAGE THAT MIGHT BE SPAM. At the least, opening the message can open the door to a flood of messages from the same sender. At worst, the message could allow a virus to sneak into your computer.

NEVER, EVER, OPEN AN ATTACHMENT TO A SPAM MESSAGE. Attachments are hackers' and virus-makers' primary means of getting access to your computer.

INSTALL A FIREWALL AND A VIRUS PROTECTION PROGRAM. A firewall is software that protects your computer from unauthorized access. If you're using a personal computer or laptop, you'll need a good firewall, along with a good virus-protection program. Be sure to keep your virus-protection program up-to-date.

A QUICK LOOK AT E-MAIL TERMINOLOGY

There are so many words and phrases related to e-mail that we can list only a few of the most common. To find a definition of an unfamiliar term that we haven't listed, type "Define: [term]" (without the quote marks) into a search engine such as Google.

Archive Store e-mail messages that need to be kept but don't need to be readily accessible.

ASCII "American Standard Code for Information Interchange." Pronounced "ass-key." A standard set of codes used for representing text, graphics, and keyboard-control characters for computer use. An ASCII file is a plain-text file that should be readable on any type of computer.

Attachment A computer file of any type that is appended to and sent with an e-mail message.

Autoresponder A computer program that automatically sends a prewritten reply to an e-mail message.

BCC "Blind Carbon Copy." The field in an e-mail header that lets you send a copy of an e-mail to one or more people without the knowledge of the people whose addresses are on the TO and CC lines; the BCC line can also be used to send a message to a group without disclosing everyone's addresses.

Bounced message An e-mail that is returned to the sender because it can't be delivered. A message might bounce back to the sender because the e-mail address is incorrect or the recipient's mailbox is full.

Browser A software program such as Netscape, Mozilla, or Internet Explorer that is used to access and view Web pages.

CC "Carbon Copy." The field in an e-mail header that lets you send a copy of an e-mail to one or more people.

Challenge-Response A method of cutting down on spam by authenticating the sender. To prove that an e-mail was sent by a person, not by an automated system, senders must respond to an e-mail challenge message before their messages are delivered.

Digital signature A unique encrypted digital code that is attached to electronically transmitted data to guarantee the authenticity of the sender.

Distribution list A group of recipients who are addressed as a single recipient.

Download The process of transferring files from one computer to another or from an Internet server to a computer's hard drive.

Emoticon Keyboard letters and symbols used to convey emotion, gestures, or expressions in an e-mail message. Also called "smileys." Not recommended for professional e-mail.

Encryption The process by which an e-mail is encoded so it can be read only by someone with the key to the code.

FAQ "Frequently asked questions." A list of answers to common questions about a particular topic.

Filter An e-mail function used to sort e-mail messages automatically.

Firewall Specialized hardware or software that prevents unauthorized access to or from a computer or network. Like the fire doors that keep a fire from spreading in a building, a firewall helps keep potentially destructive messages from entering your computer. The firewall examines each message and blocks those that do not meet specified security criteria.

Flame An e-mail that is an angry, often offensive, personal attack.

Google it The name of today's most popular search engine transformed into a verb that describes the action of using a search engine to find information.

Hard copy A printout of an e-mail message, attachment, or other document.

Header The section at the top of an e-mail that shows who sent the message, who received copies, the subject, and other information, such as the time and date the message was sent, the message size, and whether there is an attachment.

Host A computer that provides services to other "client" computers on a network, processing e-mail, serving Web pages, and running applications.

IMAP "Internet Message Access Protocol." A method that programs such as Outlook and Netscape use to send e-mail to and receive it from an e-mail server.

Instant messaging Also known as "IM." Allows you to exchange messages with any of the people on a "buddy" or contact list (when those people are on line) by typing your message into a small window that you and your buddy can both can see.

Intranet A private network of computers inside a company or organization.

IP address "Internet Protocol address." A computer's unique address, a series of four numbers separated by periods (123.45.678.10) that identifies a computer to the Internet so that information gets where it's supposed to go.

Junk mail *See* Spam, below.

Macro A text file containing a sequence of commands that can be executed by simply typing the macro's name. Useful for automating tedious and oft-repeated tasks or making it faster to enter data.

MIME "Multipurpose Internet Mail Extensions." Information incorporated into Web server and browser software that enables the automatic recognition and display of registered file types so users can exchange text, audio, or visual files.

Netiquette E-mail and Internet etiquette—the unwritten rules for using e-mail and the Internet in a way that is friendly, polite, considerate, and nonoffensive.

Phishing A form of identity theft that uses e-mail "bait" to "hook" victims. Scammers send out millions of bogus e-mail messages that appear to come from legitimate companies and sometimes refer recipients to phony Web sites that are replicas of real company sites. The scammers' goal is to trick people into revealing their passwords, Social Security numbers, credit card and bank account numbers, and other personal information.

Plain Text Plain text (ASCII) includes no formatting elements, so it can be used to transmit e-mail that any e-mail program can read.

POP "Post Office Protocol." An older method that an e-mail program uses to communicate with an e-mail server.

PPP "Point-to-Point Protocol." A protocol that allows a computer to access the Internet via a telephone line and modem.

Protocol The set of formal rules that two computers must follow to exchange messages.

Search engine A system for finding information on the Web.

Server A computer or device on a network that responds to requests for data, e-mail, file transfers, and other services from multiple "client" computers.

SMTP "Simple Mail Transfer Protocol." A set of rules governing the interaction between a program sending e-mail and a program receiving it.

Snail Mail Mail sent through the postal service (or a delivery service such as Federal Express or UPS).

Spam Unsolicited junk e-mail sent to large numbers of people. Spam is the name of a processed meat product sold by the Hormel Corporation. The use of the term to describe junk mail comes from a Monty Python skit in which the actors used the word over and over again.

Spamblock A text block inserted between the "@" and the domain name in an e-mail address in order to prevent people from collecting the actual address and using it to send SPAM. Any e-mail sent to an address that includes the spamblock will automatically bounce back to the sender as undeliverable.

Surf Navigate from page to page on the Web.

TCP/IP "Transmission Control Protocol/Internet Protocol." Two of the main protocols or sets of rules that allow a computer to be connected to the Internet.

Thread A series of messages in an ongoing e-mail conversation.

URL "Uniform Resource Locator." The address of a file or Web page that is accessible on the Internet (http://www.writeitwell.com).

Virus A potentially destructive software program, macro, or fragment of code that can be spread through e-mail and attachments.

Web "World Wide Web." A network of servers linked by a common protocol that allows computer users to access and distribute text, graphics, and multimedia information to users all over the world.

Worm A self-contained software program (or set of programs) that can replicate itself as it spreads from computer to computer, often clogging networks and information systems. Worms can be delivered in e-mail messages or attachments.

Zip file One or more files that have been compressed to save storage and download more quickly.

READINGS AND RESOURCES

See our Web site for checklists, helpful links, and other resources, including writing tips and training guides.

ABOUT THE AUTHOR

The author of books and self-study guides on writing and other topics, Janis Fisher Chan has been developing training programs and conducting classroom training for more than 25 years. Her focus is on providing practical techniques and concepts that people can use immediately to communicate clearly and work well with others.

In addition to *E-Mail: A Write It Well Guide* and other books in the Write It Well series, she has written several self-study training programs for the American Management Association, including *Managing Your Priorities, Making Successful Presentations, Communication Skills for Managers (5th edition), Successful Delegating for Managers,* and *Managing Your Priorities.* For Wiley, she wrote *An Academic Manager's Guide to Meetings* and served as developmental editor for the highly acclaimed *Leadership Challenge* series, *The Five Dysfunctions of a Team* Workshop Kit, and other training packages and books. She recently designed and developed a three-day Leadership Development Program for Wiley managers.

ABOUT WRITE IT WELL

Write It Well began business in 1979 as Advanced Communication Designs, Inc., a training company that specialized in helping people communicate clearly and work together effectively. Our focus has always been on providing practical information, techniques, and strategies that people can use immediately. Our books and training programs are used by individuals, teams, training specialists, and instructors in corporations and businesses of all sizes, nonprofit organizations, government agencies, and colleges and universities.

The Write It Well series currently includes *Just Commas* and the self-paced training workbooks, *Professional Writing Skills, How to Write Reports and Proposals, Grammar for Grownups,* and *Writing Performance Documentation.* For more about our company and detailed descriptions of our publications, visit our Web site, www.writeitwell.com.

ENDNOTES

[1]Samantha Finnegan and Wilson Cleveland, "80% of Users Prefer E-Mail as Business Communication Tool, Says META Group," April 22, 2003, www.metagroup.com

[2]www.amanet.org/research and www.raticati.com

[3]*Webster's New Collegiate Dictionary*, G. C. Merriam Co., 1977

[4]Edward M. Hallowell, MD, "Overloaded Circuits, Why Smart People Underperform," *Harvard Business Review*, January, 2005

[5]William Strunk, Jr., and E. B. White, *The Elements of Style, Third Edition*, MacMillan Publishing Co., Inc., 1979

[6]*Webster's New Collegiate Dictionary*

NOTES

NOTES

NOTES

NOTES

NOTES

NOTES